# THE SOCIAL THOUGHT OF BERNARD MANDEVILLE

# THE SOCIAL THOUGHT OF BERNARD MANDEVILLE

*Virtue and Commerce in Early Eighteenth-Century England*

THOMAS A. HORNE

New York   Columbia University Press   1978

The Andrew W. Mellon Foundation, through a special grant, has assisted Columbia University Press in publishing this volume.

*Published in 1978 in Great Britain by*
*The Macmillan Press Ltd.*
*and in the United States of America by*
*Columbia University Press.*

*Printed in Great Britain*

**Library of Congress Cataloging in Publication Data**

**Horne, Thomas A.**
   **The social thought of Bernard Mandeville.**

   **Bibliography: p.**
   **Includes index.**
   **1. Mandeville, Bernard, 1670–1733.   2. Self-**
**interest.   3. Mercantilism.   I. Title.**
**HM22.G8M354   1977          300.1          77-23573**
**ISBN 0–231–04274–4**

TO E. T. R. and K. C. H.

# Contents

# Preface

I have been fortunate to have studied and worked with many people who were kind and patient enough to pass on to me ideas and attitudes I have found indispensable. Among those I would particularly like to thank are Professor Peter Bachrach of Temple University, Professor Milton Cummings of The Johns Hopkins University, and Mr. David Wise.

I discovered Mandeville in a seminar taught by Professor Julian Franklin and I would like to thank him and Professor Herbert Deane for their guidance throughout graduate school as well as their all too justified criticisms of this manuscript. Professor Maurice Goldsmith of the University of Exeter was kind enough to bring the *Female Tatler* and the Reformation of Manners to my attention. Mr. Jesse Goodale provided thoughtful comments on chapters 1 and 2. Most of all, I would like to thank my wife, Kathryn, for her help and infinite patience.

The reader will note that the capitalization has been modernized in all quotations from the seventeenth and eighteenth centuries.

# Introduction

Until the eighteenth century, there was a general (though not un-
animous) agreement among social theorists that the proper operation
of the social organism depended upon the wide dispersion throughout
society of virtue – most generally, the ability to recognize a public interest and act upon it – and that the goal of any social organization had
to be the creation and nurturing of virtuous men. It was also generally
agreed that economic activity, unless strictly limited, constituted the
most dangerous threat to the virtuous life. While virtue depended upon
the willingness to adopt a public stance, commercial activity tended to
change legitimate concerns for the self into selfishness, to enlarge
private concerns and diminish the awareness of public needs. Bernard
Mandeville, writing in the first years of the eighteenth century, and
fully aware of the conflict between virtue and commerce, still chose
without flinching the world of commerce. Because of this choice he was
driven to develop a wholly nonmoral interpretation of social organization and development. Moreover, his particular formulation of the antagonism between virtue and commerce deeply influenced English
social theorists of the eighteenth century and compelled them to find
new ways of thinking about their society.

The early eighteenth century in England was acutely aware of the
importance of virtue in society and government through the strength of
a tradition – now generally referred to as civic humanism[1] –
particularly active at the time. The 1688 revolution, thought by some to
be a moral as well as a political revolution, the anxiety caused by the
death of Anne and the establishment of the House of Hanover in 1714,
the continued strength of the Jacobites which seemed to threaten the
stability of England, and the South Sea Bubble of 1720 with Robert
Walpole's attempt to screen those responsible – all occasioned renewed
stress on the importance of virtue and public spiritedness for the continued cohesion of society. At the same time, early eighteenth-century
England witnessed considerable economic changes, which seemed to
many to be corrupting influences.[2] Moreover, this period faced the

problem of a large, idle, surplus population – seen by many as political-
ly unstable and economically unproductive – which seemed to require
the introduction of moral discipline.

The two primary categories of civic humanism, virtue and corruption, had their origins in the modern world in the thought of Niccolò
Machiavelli, especially in his work *The Discourses*. The tradition passed
into English thought during the English Civil War in the works of
James Harrington and later in the century in the works of men like
Algernon Sidney. In the early eighteenth century John Trenchard and
Thomas Gordon carried on the tradition in their *Cato's Letters*, written in
1720–23, which held before their readers the glory of the Roman republic that "conquered by its virtue more than its arms . . ."[3] and the
fall of that republic because of magnificence, luxury, and pride, which
corrupted the manners of the people. The polemics of Trenchard and
Gordon were clearly directed against the ministry of Robert Walpole.
They were joined in their attack on Walpole by Tory writers such as
Bolingbroke, John Gay, and Jonathan Swift, who, if they did not share
all of the religious and republican ideas of the Real Whigs, did
share their hatred of Walpole and their concern with corruption and
virtue.[4]

The distance between those who maintained the moral interpretation of social life and Mandeville is apparent when we consider that
at the same time that moral reformers, through the Societies for the
Reformation of Manners, were helping to arrest men for drinking on
Sundays, Mandeville published in 1724 "A Modest Defense of Publick
Stews," which recommended setting up one hundred legal houses of
prostitution employing two thousand "ladies of easy virtue." And in
the same year of the scandal of the South Sea Bubble, 1720, when Walpole was vituperatively attacked as a "skreen," Mandeville wrote:

> When we shall have carefully examined the state of our affairs, and
> so far conquered our prejudices as not to suffer ourselves to be delud-
> ed any longer by false appearances, the prospect of happiness will be
> before us. To expect ministries without faults, and courts without
> vices is grossly betraying our ignorance of human affairs. Nothing
> under the sun is perfect.[5]

Mandeville's most characteristic attack on the philosophy of
public-spiritedness was that it did not understand human nature and
the true motive which moved men – self-interest. However, the importance of Mandeville is not his recognition of self-interest; rather, it is his
attempt to provide a coherent theory of society's development and
operation based entirely on the self-interested actions of men without
recourse to moral forces. Mandeville's view is perfectly summarized in
his statement that

Men are naturally selfish, unruly creatures, what makes them sociable is their necessity and consciousness of standing in need of others' help to make life comfortable: and what makes this assistance voluntary and lasting are the gains on profit accrueing to industry for services done to others, which in a well ordered society enables every body, who in some thing or other will be serviceable to the publick, to purchase the assistance of others.[6]

The total rejection by Mandeville of the categories of virtue and public-spiritedness, which constituted the most characteristic way of thinking about society in early eighteenth-century England, his substitution of self-interest and commercial wealth for these categories, and an inquiry into mercantilism and the moral ideas that surrounded and led from Jansenism as the sources upon which he drew, constitute the subject of this book. Chapter 1 considers the Societies for the Reformation of Manners as the immediate impetus to Mandeville's work and documents his opposition to these societies. Chapter 2 seeks to find the origins of some of Mandeville's ideas in the traditions of French moral thought. Chapter 3 focuses on his own alternative view of society as it was developed against the work of the third Earl of Shaftesbury. Chapter 4 provides the economic context of his thought and presents his views on economics and his prescription for national wealth. Chapter 5 considers the reaction of his contemporaries, both in the more obscure pamphlet literature and in the work of more substantial critics such as Francis Hutcheson and David Hume, and the process by which the antagonism in Mandeville's thought between virtue and commerce is overcome by these writers.

Surprisingly little is known about Mandeville's life even though his works generated enormous controversy and gained him considerable fame. The most complete account of his life can be found in the introduction of F. B. Kaye's edition of *The Fable of the Bees*.[7] Bernard Mandeville was born in 1670 in Rotterdam. He attended the Erasmus School in that city until 1685 when he enrolled in the University of Leyden. There he studied philosophy and medicine, receiving in 1691 the degree of Doctor of Medicine. His practice specialized in nerve and stomach disorders, the same field in which his father had worked.

In the middle 1690s he took a tour of Europe, which ended in a stay in London to learn the English language. He found "the country and the manners of it agreeable to his humour," married in 1698/9, and remained in England until his death.

Mandeville was apparently a prosperous physician on familiar terms with Sir Hans Sloane, the founder of the Royal Society, and the Earl of Macclesfield, an early member of Walpole's government who left in a scandal in 1725. One of the few glimpses of Mandeville's life is found in Benjamin Franklin's *Autobiography*. He describes meeting Mandeville this way:

My pamphlet by some means falling into the hands of one Lyons, a surgeon . . . it occasioned an acquaintance between us; he took great notice of me, called on me often to converse on those subjects, carried me to the Horns, a pale ale house in ———— Lane, Cheapside, and introduced me to Dr. Mandeville, author of "The Fable of the Bees," who had a club there of which he was the soul, being a most facetious, entertaining companion.[8]

In 1732/3 Mandeville died.

# Chapter 1 Mandeville and the Reformation of Manners

In the middle of the 1690s, when Bernard Mandeville arrived in London after a trip through Europe, he found in progress an organized attempt to reform the rough manners and curb the "abominable impieties [which] had overspread the nation."[1] The work of the Societies for the Reformation of Manners forms the background to Mandeville's early writings and remained an antagonist that concerned him, to a greater or lesser degree, for the rest of his life.

The first society was established about 1690 in the Tower-Hamlets in London when certain laymen decided to organize in order to suppress the "bawdy-houses" which were, they felt, breeding grounds for many kinds of crime. The author of an early tract championing the movement recounts the founding of the society this way.

> ... the officers and inhabitants of the Tower-Hamlets, upon occasion of their majesties proclamation for the apprehending of highway-men, robbers etc. considering that common bawdy-houses were the usual nurseries and receptacles of sick evil people, resolved to use their utmost diligence and endeavors to suppress the same; and for that purpose drew up an agreement in writing ....[2]

Twenty-five years later another anonymous pamphleteer, in recalling the start of the societies, averred that " God was pleased to put into the hearts of five or six private gentlemen, of the Church of England ... measures for a resolute stand against that dreadful and general corruption of morals."[3] Soon after the original society was formed one of its founders moved to the Strand where he started another group. By 1699 eight more groups had organized and by 1701 there were about twenty societies in England.

The great cry of the societies was for a vigorous and magnanimous prosecution of the ends of these laws, which is the suppression of all wickedness and impiety."[4] The belief that the strict enforcement of the laws by the proper magistrate would be enough to curb vice quickly and establish a virtuous England can be seen in Josiah Woodward's

1

statement "that constables have a great power for the suppression of prophaneness and debauchery, and that if they would conscientiously exercise it . . . and private persons would more generally give information against prophane and vicious men, we might in a very little time see a reformation of manners . . ."[5] Woodward, the chief publicist of the societies, included in his *A Help to a National Reformation containing . . . An Account of the Progress of the Reformation of Manners*, which was first published in 1699 and became virtually a handbook for the societies, a list of the existing laws against moral offenses. Even as late as 1729 when the influence of the societies had greatly waned, a work was published to lend weight to "putting the laws in execution against immorality and profaneness [which was] the glorious design of the Societies for the Reformation of Manners."[6] The author of this book brought together all the laws against immoral acts that he could find in ancient societies up to the eleventh century in Europe.

In order to gain the strict enforcement of the laws against immorality, much of this writing was directed toward magistrates. Thus, there are sections in Woodward's book on "Obligations of a Justice of the Peace" and "Oaths and Obligations of a Constable."[7] However, the emphasis of the movement was directed toward gaining the active involvement of the members of the societies.

The English legal system in this period relied upon information given by private individuals and this procedure made it possible for a group like the Societies for the Reformation of Manners to become actively involved in law enforcement. According to a student of this period, "a private person could obtain a warrant from a Justice of the Peace or Magistrate, sometimes on his unsupported evidence, and this warrant of conviction the constable of the parish was required to execute."[8] After the convicted persons paid a fine or served a term in jail they could sue for false charges, but if they lost they had to pay treble costs. The societies, with the help of friendly magistrates, distributed blank warrants to its members, who filled in the names of wrongdoers, and collected the filled-in warrants to return them to the magistrates.

A sense of the reformers' zeal can be gathered from Woodward, who suggested that the members and their sympathizers

> . . . exert their power, in going about into the streets, markets, and other public places, on weekdays, for the taking up of drunkards, swearers, etc. and carrying them before magistrates; and on the Lords day, by inspecting into public houses, for the preventing of tipling; and by the taking up of drovers, carriers, etc. that travel on that day, and such as carry their wares or goods about the streets to their customers, or are found at unlawful sports and pastimes, as they are directed in the help to Reformation.[9]

It appears, however, that the members of the society were rarely informers themselves, but employed others to inform for a fee. The practice of informing was no more popular then than it is now, and the informer soon became the symbol of the societies to their enemies.[10]

The defenders of the societies all attempted to blunt this criticism. Woodward included a set of directions and warnings to informers which cautioned them to "give no information when a matter of fact is doubtful" and provided certain methods to determine, for example, if a man was drunk or had simply lost his balance.[11] William Bisset in his published sermons tried to justify the practice of informing by arguing "that he who heareth cursing and betrayeth it not, is as deep in the guilt as he who is a partner with a thief or privy to his unlawful practices, and will not discover them."[12] The nature of these criticisms against the societies, as well as one possible defense, can be seen from Isaac Watts's sermon delivered to the societies in 1707: "They say ye are busy-bodies . . . ye are but assistants to the magistrate in that work . . . . They cry upon you as severe and cruel . . . . Here I am bold to answer for you, that it is uneasy and self-denying work, and that you had rather be employed in propagating virtue by milder methods if they might but obtain success."[13]

The origin of the movement for the reformation of manners can be found in the religious revival that occurred under the short reign of James II. "One way to show a stubborn defiance of James' rule was to throng to the churches and chapels of England."[14] The Glorious Revolution of 1688 added further impetus to the movement because it was perceived by many as a moral as well as a political revolution. One pamphleteer, for example, believed that Charles II and James II encouraged vice to further their tyrannical designs and that the revolution which brought William and Mary to the throne "was an opportunity put into our power when we might have effected a thorough Reformation."[15] King William lent his weight to the movement when, in a letter to the bishop of London on February 13, 1689, he wrote:

> We must earnestly desire and shall endeavor a general reformation of manners of all our subjects as being that which must establish our throne and secure to our people their religion, happiness and peace, all which seem to be in great danger at this time by reason of that overflowing of vice which is too notorious in this as well as other neighboring nations.[16]

Despite misgivings about the societies, William issued two more proclamations on this subject. Anne continued the practice to such an extent that Isaac Watts likened her to Moses in a "British Israel."[17]

Another manifestation of this religious revival can be seen in the founding of the Society for Promoting Christian Knowledge. While they limited their membership to members of the Anglican Church, unlike the Societies for the Reformation of Manners, which included dissenters as well as the orthodox, they too were interested in improving the manners of the period. These societies, founded in 1698/9, though they distributed Woodward's book on the reformation of manners, took a different tack in the effort for moral improvement. They concerned themselves primarily with setting up and running Charity Schools.[18] Because the methods of the reforming societies stirred up opposition which cost them support, the Charity School movement became the main vehicle of moral improvement in the first years of the eighteenth century.

The extent of the reforming societies' activity can be gathered from the twentieth edition (1721) of their practical handbook, *Help to a National Reformation*. In that volume they claim to have prompted two thousand prosecutions for moral offenses in the past year and 75,270 since 1691. In the 1738 edition of the book, the last edition published, they recorded 101,683 prosecutions in the years after the founding of the societies. While these claims cannot be completely believed, it seems clear that the reforming societies were a major social force in the last part of the seventeenth century and the first part of the eighteenth century. They exerted enough influence to worry both the king and the established church, which were suspicious of any attempt to deal with moral reformation and religious revival outside the already existing structures.[19] Thus, for example, Henry Sacheverell first rose to fame by attacking the societies.[20]

Throughout the literature of the movement for reform ran one common theme – the public necessity of controlling private immorality. While this theme was not at all new, it took on an added significance in this period of English history because of concern for the recent political and religious establishment and the fear of Jacobite rebellion. At the same time, the early eighteenth century experienced the chaotic growth of urban centers, especially London, which created horrid living conditions.[21] Current economic doctrines, which stressed the need for a well-disciplined labor force, lent impetus to the reform movement. Finally, there was a middle class that was able to organize and systematically carry out reforms in a way that touched the lives of many people.[22]

The literature of the societies began from the assumption that morality was identical to religion and that the virtue to be gained through religious belief was the cement which held society together. Thus, an anonymous pamphleteer began his *A Representation of the State of the Societies for a Reformation of Manners* by stating that "there is not a maxim more just in any politics whatever, than that prophaneness and debauchery are the worst enemies to a state."[23] Isaac Watts was even more explicit about the effects of sin upon the public in his sermon to the societies in 1701.

The public affairs of a nation must suffer certain detriment where wickedness roves loose and unrestrained. If the flood gates of sin are opened, confusion will rush into the government like a deluge. Men that break the bonds of natural religion and morality without control, will grow lawless and ungovernable . . . . they will stand at defiance with the best of governments . . . . they are ready for insurrection and public tumult.[24]

The precise relationship between private sin and public calamity was never made perfectly clear because, in part, the assumption was widespread and simply obvious to the vast majority of the people. However, the most general charges brought against private vices were that they undermined that system of subordination upon which the social order was based and that they destroyed the concern for the public which was especially important in a republic. Vices such as pride, envy, and ambition could cause a man to try to leave his proper status and aspire to something higher for which he was not suited. Other vices could affect the social order from the opposite direction. Luxury, gaming, or drunkenness could ruin the fortunes of a great family. A favorite target for the reformers in this regard was masked balls.[25] These ceremonies allowed men to appear to be something they were not, a serious offense in a society that clung "to rigid demarcations between class and class."[26]

Proper concern for the public weal could be destroyed by any number of vices. Avarice, luxury, or pride could each cause a man to put his own private gain above the welfare of the country. While these vices were dangerous in private citizens, they were doubly dangerous in magistrates. In the reformers' eyes, party strife and faction were a particularly important result of the profusion of vice and the preference for self over the public interest. The economic well-being of the country also depended upon the absence of certain vices. Idleness was of great concern because of the effects it could have on the productive power of the nation. Because of the common identification of the family with the nation, all of those vices that could ruin the financial fortune of a family were thought to be ruinous to the nation's wealth.

The long history of the belief in the necessity to curb private vice for the well-being of the nation was not lost on the reformers, who used it to support their arguments. We have already seen that Josiah Woodward believed that the control of vice "hath . . . ever been thought the great interest and business of government."[27] But we can find more sophisticated tracts, which not only assert the long tradition of controlling private acts, but also contain a historical inquiry into the activities of earlier governments to prove their case. In 1704 James Whiston introduced his analysis of *England's State . . . Distempers* by considering the reasons for the decline of earlier states. He began with a commonplace statement:

> Who ever hath made observations of the general transactions and af-
> fairs of the world must of necessity be sensible that all the
> revolutions of empires . . . that have degenerated from better to
> worse, have derived their misfortunes from the decay of religion, vir-
> tue, and common justice.
>
> The true observance of which is the bond and cement of all
> societies, however founded or regulated.[28]

Whiston then examined the Greek city-states and found that it was the "epidemical debauchery, and the abominable corruption of the magistracy infecting people that destroyed the many flourishing cities of the Grecian Empire."[29] Moreover, the strength of the Lacedemonians could be explained through their ability to maintain their virtue. We are not surprised when he states so matter of factly that even "they who have but nibbled at the margin of history, knows that the unreproved, and unrestrained dissoluteness of their [Roman] manners, was the original ground of all their [Roman] intestine convulsions and disorders, giving thereby opportunity to Pompey and Caesar . . . ."[30]

A quarter of a century later John Disney produced what must be the apex of this argument in *A View of Ancient Laws against Immorality and Profaneness*. In order to prove "that it is the business of laws and magistrates, to punish the licentious morals of a people, as well as rapine, theft, sedition, murder, or any other enormity,"[31] he listed in chapters on each vice (Adultery, Gaming, Drunkenness, etc.) all the laws he could find in the ancient kingdoms and medieval Christian world that made these vices illegal.

The pamphlet by Whiston is also useful in illustrating another argument against private vice, namely, the relationship between widespread vice and arbitrary power. In the same way that Pompey and Caesar were able to come to power because of widespread debauchery, an arbitrary ruler would be the outcome of a degeneration in English moral behavior. Whiston believed that Charles II and James II discouraged morality and virtue and encouraged vice in order to facilitate their plans for arbitrary power. Thus "idleness, luxury, debauchery, prophaneness, and deism are the builders and supporters of arbitrary power . . . ."[32] The close association between arbitrary power, "the slavish doctrine of passive obedience,"[33] and popery meant that the religious as well as the political establishment in Great Britain was dependent upon a virtuous citizenry. In the minds of many Englishmen of this time it was clear that the Pope, Charles, and the French had been allied with the devil in the attempt to subvert the morals of Englishmen. These attitudes have been historically associated primarily with the Whigs, so that it is not surprising that it was assumed at the time that all members of the Societies for the Reformation of Manners were Whigs and low churchmen, and that most of their opposition came from high churchmen, such as Sacheverell.

One further belief of the period, which the reformers used, was that vice risked bringing down the judgment of God. It was conceivable to many in the early eighteenth century that He would punish England for its vices. Isaac Watts preached that God commanded men to fight against sin and reminded Englishmen of the fate of Sodom and Gomorrah.[34] William Bisset emphasized the idea of a jealous God and warned that vice "draws such a load of guilt on our souls and . . . such a load of divine wrath and judgement on our heads . . . ."[35] The slight earthquake experienced by London in 1692 and the great storm of 1703 were both taken as signs of God's anger. Richard Willis summarized this view when he stated: "National sins deserve national judgements."[36]

The year Dean Willis uttered these words in support of a national reformation, Mandeville published in a pamphlet a long poem in which he makes his first mention of the reforming societies. He describes an earlier period of "peace and plenty" that

Had no reformers, under banners
of holy thrift-encountering manners.
Those champions of sobriety,
That watch to keep the world a dry. . .
I say twas in that wicked time,
when quenching thirst was thought no crime.[37]

The next year Mandeville published anonymously a sixpenny pamphlet entitled *The Grumbling Hive: or, Knaves Turned Honest*. The pamphlet must have met with some success because it was soon pirated and sold about the streets of London.[38] This short bit of doggerel, written in Hudibrastic verse, was a satirical attack upon the ideas and efforts then associated with the Societies for the Reformation of Manners.

Mandeville does not differ with the societies in their perception that vice, corruption, and fraud are widespread. In fact, Mandeville is even more unrelenting in his examination of vice in the London of the period. The "Millions endeavoring to supply/Each others' lust and vanity"[39] encompassed not only the obvious frauds such as "Sharpers, parasites, pimps, players,/Pick-pockets, coiners, quacks, sooth-sayers," but, according to Mandeville, "the grave industrious were the same." (p.19). The art of lawyers rested on raising feuds, physicians cared more about money than their patients' health, and even the priests were only those "that could hide / Their sloth, lust, avarice and pride" (p. 21).

However, while "every part was full of vice,/Yet the whole mass a paradise" (p. 24). The hive was materially wealthy and militarily strong. Moreover, this strength was not in spite of widespread vice, but because of it.

> . . . . . . . . . . . . . . . . . . . whilst luxury
> Employed a million of the poor,
> And odious pride a million more:
> Envy itself, and vanity,
> Were ministers of industry;
> Their darling folly, fickleness,
> In diet, furniture and dress,
> That strange ridiculous vice, was made
> The very wheel that turned the trade [p. 25].

It was only because men had an inordinate desire for money, over-valued themselves, cared how they appeared in their neighbors' eyes, and desired to outstrip others in ostentation that they worked hard and created the wealth that the country enjoyed. In this way

> Their crimes conspired to make them great:
> And virtue, who from politiks
> Had learned a thousand cunning tricks,
> Was, by this happy influence,
> Made friends with vice . . . [p. 24].

The bees refused to be satisfied with their situation and, in what must be a clear reference to the societies, bewailed the existence of vice. Hypocritically ". . . everyone cry'd damn the cheats / and would, tho' conscious of his own, / In others barberously bear none" (p. 26). Others preached ". . . the land must sink / for all its fraud" (p. 27). Angered by this hypocrisy, Jove decided to grant these pleas and bestow on the hive universal honesty.

It is not difficult to imagine what Mandeville foresees for the hive. Lawyers, jailers, and smiths (who made locks) were soon out of work. Because all the bees were now satisfied with simple houses and clothes, vanity and pride having been banished, those who made a living supplying these needs were also out of work. In short, the economy collapsed because "Content [is] the bane of industry" (p. 34). The hive, no longer concerned with the "empty glory got by wars" (p. 32), ceased to maintain a large army and was quickly attacked and defeated by a less honest neighbor.

If we read this work of Mandeville's in the light of the work of the reforming societies, we see that the moral which ends *The Grumbling Hive* is Mandeville's prescription to the reformers.

> Then leave complaints: Fools only strive
> To make a great an honest hive.
> T'enjoy the worlds conveniences,
> Be famed in war, yet live in ease,

Without great vices, is a vain
Eutopia seated in the brain.
Fraud, luxury and pride must live,
While we the benefits receive... [p. 36].

The first volume of *The Fable of the Bees* begins with this poem and the rest of the book is organized as extended comments on the various lines and phrases that it contains. *The Grumbling Hive* includes in an adumbrated form most of the ideas that will occupy Mandeville throughout his literary career. There is, first of all, the perception of almost universal egoism. Mandeville is specific in characterizing even the most honorable professionals – doctors, lawyers, and clergymen – as primarily self-interested. One manifestation of this self-centeredness is men's tendency to overrate themselves, engaging in much self-delusion and hypocrisy. Men damn the vices they see in others while ignoring those same vices in themselves, and it is this capacity for delusion which enables them to envision "vain eutopias." One of the major motifs in all of Mandeville's work is his attempt to see through these delusions. Once he has unmasked man it becomes possible to apprehend the real springs of his actions and the real bases of society. The most famous and infamous of Mandeville's doctrines – private vices, public virtues – is understood after society has been forced to look at itself honestly. Then we see that those things which were thought to be vicious by early eighteenth-century moralists were precisely the passions that contributed to material well-being. It was not self-centeredness that had to be expunged, but the refusal to accept that egoism and to use it in such a way as to make virtue friends with vice. The opinion that we see so often in the pamphlets of the reformers that the cement of society was religious virtue, gives way in Mandeville to the idea that it is mutual need and want which lie at the base of society's cohesion.

Mandeville's opposition to the reforming societies and their spirit is clearly expressed in a number of other enterprises. On Tuesday, April 12, 1709, the first issue of Richard Steele's journal, the *Tatler*, appeared. Its tremendous success served as an example to other aspiring essayists who quickly copied the format and often used the title in their own work. One of these was the *Female Tatler*, in the beginning written by a "Mrs. Crackenthorpe, a lady that knows everything," which first appeared on July 8, 1709. But in issue number 52, Mrs. Crackenthorpe gave way to "a Society of Ladies." It now appears that one of the writers behind the society was Bernard Mandeville.[40]

It seems appropriate that Mandeville would use the *Tatler* as a foil because it symbolizes much of the effort to convert England to more polite manners. The original dedication of the *Tatler* straightforwardly states:

The general purpose of this paper is to expose the false arts of life, to pull off the disguises of cunning, vanity, and affectation, and to recommend a general simplicity in our dress, our discourse, and our behavior.[41]

In issue number 3 the authors are explicit about the relationship of this task to the movement to reform manners. Bickerstaff, Steele's fictional spokesman, at first hints of his feeling toward the reformers when, in disagreeing with their opposition to the theater, he still refers to them as "my friends and fellow labourers, the Reformers of Manners." But later in the same paragraph he admits outright to being an ally of the reformers and gives some examples of the sorts of behavior he will admonish.

> As I just now hinted, I own myself of the "Society for Reformation of Manners." . . . Therefore, as I design to have notices from all public assemblies, I shall take upon me only indecorums, inproprieties, and negligences, in such as should give us better examples. After this declaration, if a fine lady thinks fit to giggle at church, or a great beau comes in drunk to a play, either shall be sure to hear of it in my ensuing paper. For, merely as a well bred man, I cannot bear these enormities.[42]

The *Tatler* as the embodiment of the attempt to reform manners and encourage public-spiritedness was a target Mandeville must have found too tempting to resist.

There was no need for Mandeville or the other writers of the *Female Tatler* to be circumspect in their displeasure with the *Tatler*. Bickerstaff is frequently mentioned by name, and specific issues of the *Tatler* are cited. For example, in the *Female Tatler* of December 19, 1709 (issue 72) we are directed to the *Tatler* of the preceding Saturday (issue 108, December 11) wherein we find a passage that puts forward the intention of the *Tatler* and which clearly distinguishes for us the difference between the *Tatler* and Mandeville. Steele writes:

> Is it possible . . . that human nature can rejoice in its disgrace, and take pleasure in seeing its own figure turned to ridicule, and distorted into forms that raise horror and aversion? . . . Men of elegant and noble minds are shocked at seeing characters of persons who deserve esteem for their virtue, knowledge, or services to their country, placed in wrong lights, and by misrepresentation made the subject of buffoonery . . . . As man is a creature made up of different extremes, he has something in him very great and very mean . . . . The finest authors of antiquity have taken him on the more advantageous side. They cultivate the natural grandeur of the soul, raise in her a glorious ambition, feed her with hopes of immortality and perfection, and do all they can to widen the partition between the virtuous and the vicious.[43]

This passage, according to Mandeville, is the result of pride and vanity, which have ended in the self-delusion that he so detested. In the first line of the *Fable* Mandeville repudiates the position taken by Bickerstaff. He states: "One of the greatest reasons why so few people understand themselves, is, that most writers are always teaching men what they should be, and hardly ever trouble their heads with telling them what they really are."[44]

Throughout the articles in the *Female Tatler* we find Mandeville in his typical stance, unmasking pretensions, exposing self-interest, and arguing that virtue and vice are inextricably intertwined. His early essays are particularly concerned with showing that social progress springs not from learned public-spiritedness, but from the passions and vices of people. In issue 62 he constructs an argument in which one of the ladies, Lucinda, says that she "can never forebear thinking how infinitely we are indebted to all those that ever invented anything for the public good ... and I am of the ingenious Mr. Bickerstaff's opinion that none are to be counted alive, but such as, setting aside all private interest and personal pleasure, are generous enough to labour and exert themselves for the benefit of others."[45] It happens, however, that an "Oxford Gentleman" is present who disagrees with this analysis, and puts forward what we have come to recognize as one of Mandeville's arguments.

> Madame, said he, it is unquestionable, that the greatest and most immediate benefactors to human society, are the idle favourites of blind fortune [who] take no other care than to please themselves, and studying as well to create new appetites as to gratify those they feel already, are given over to all sensuality ....[46]

This gentleman does not believe that men came to live together because of "some good quality or innate virtue perculiar to themselves," but because of their wants, appetites, and "the vast love everyone of them has for himself." It may be, this gentleman continues, that the good of our immortal souls demands virtue, "but humility, temperance, contentedness, frugality ... are very insignificant, as to the public .... Nothing is more beneficial to the public, than the prodigal, or more immediately detrimental than the miser, yet both are vices, without which the society could not subsist. The state is upheld by contraries, and all that conduces to the common good, ought to be welcome to a true politician."[47]

In the next two issues of the *Female Tatler* Mandeville continues his disagreement with Bickerstaff's opinion that "the living are only those that are some way or another laudably employed in the improvement of their own minds, or for the advantage of others ...."[48] He examines the different learned professions – scholars, divines, lawyers, doctors – and discovers "how insignificant the lucubrations as well as the day-light labours of the learned have been in the main to human society."[49] He defends both the common tradesman and the ostentatious wealthy, "those people that take no other worldly care than how to dress, eat, drink and sleep well,"[50] as the people who have turned the wheels of trade and improved, for example, furniture, watches, and ships.

Having shown that men of learning and public spirit are less important to society than they imagine, Mandeville then sets out to consider the motivations of the honourable. In issue 80, after "Colonel Worthy" has enumerated the reasons why honor and honorable men have been esteemed, the "Oxford Gentleman" attempts to uncover the real motives of these men. Men, he begins, are contradictory. While "we are all lovers of self-preservation," we all also desire to be praised. But, because self-seeking is natural, praise is bestowed only on actions which seem to aim at another's good. The honorable act kindly not in order to help others, but only so that they may acquire praise. Thus, "if the public spirited man . . . be pleased strictly to examine himself, he will find that he has never committed any action deliberately but for his own sake."[51]

Again we can notice a theme that dominates everything that Mandeville writes; that is, that both man and society are permeated with contradiction. This theme continues in the discussion of honor in the *Female Tatler*. Men of honor "are the oddest mixture of good and evil, and for their principles the most unaccountable creatures in the world."[52] On the one hand, they show veneration in all matters religious, pay their debts, keep their friendships, and act properly toward the women they meet. Yet, inseparable from these good qualities are certain vicious ones. Chief among these is the practice among honorable men of ending all controversies according to the traditions of dueling. They put themselves above the laws of the country and imagine they are sovereigns of sorts, so that killing a man in a duel is no different for them from slaying an enemy in war.

The contradiction involving the men of honor is made even more complex because "the cunning politician . . . [who] . . . disposes of every part of the society to the best advantage" does not try to cure them of their dual nature. The politician who understands their importance to maintaining the peace of the country "has never contradicted their ridiculous notions." Instead, he plays on their enormous vanity and is able to pay for their services with "nothing but empty praise."[53] Mandeville has tried to show that the men of honor, who form an important part of the public–spirited, act from self-interest like all other men, are a mixture of good and evil, and can be used by a skillful politician for the public good.

In the last few issues of the *Female Tatler* Mandeville turns his attention to an idea that he found used by the *Tatler* in the effort to reform manners: public-spiritedness is the only way to happiness and content-ment. He is made angry "with those people that would prescribe rules of happiness to everybody else,"[54] and instead believes that "there is no general definition to be given of happiness."[55]

To defend the rewards that can be found in a private life un-concerned with public affairs, Mandeville presents the reader with the case of Laborio, a rich, avaricious merchant who, in spite of his age and wealth, still rises at five every morning. Laborio loves the pursuit and pleasures of money, regardless of what philosophers say, and has learn-ed "that we are all very unequitable judges of one another's pleasures."[56]

Much of the writing found in the *Tatler* seems to extol the characteristics we normally associate with an aristocracy or with a middle class trying to ape the aristocracy by presenting an ideal picture of itself. When Bickerstaff avers that the "calm and elegant satisfaction which the vulgar call melancholy is the true end and proper delight of men of knowledge," and that "the pleasures of ordinary people are in their passions; but the seat of this delight is in the reason and understanding,"[57] we are in a world different from that of the Laborios who populate and find justification in Mandeville's work. Mandeville has little interest in "calm and elegant satisfaction" and argues that philosophic contentment is not for mortals. While it is possible to be happy in one's station, each station has its own anxieties and troubles. Thus, Mandeville concludes

> that content in its limited sense is very commendable, but that the other is only a pretence to a chimera, and a romantick notion that has no other parents than haughtiness and self-conceit; and that a great many people, that end their days in the pursuit of wealth, and have in reality no other delight than what my sister called the toil of life, receive more inward satisfaction, and enjoy greater happiness in the midst of noise and hurry, than others, that retiring themselves from the world, boast their content with so much arrogance.[58]

Contentment is "the bane of industry,"[59] and Mandeville will seek to debunk it whenever he can.

While the *Female Tatler* provided Mandeville with an opportunity to criticize Steele's variant of the reformation of manners, the format never enabled Mandeville to launch a long, more penetrating critique. In the first edition of the *Fable* in 1714, Mandeville begins with a short essay entitled "An Enquiry into the Origins of Moral Virtue," which sets out his alternative to the reforming ideology of "the incomparable Sir Richard Steele."[60]

Mandeville begins by stating that his interest is man as he really is and not as some would like him to be. Against the kind of view uttered by Bickerstaff that "There is nothing which I contemplate with greater pleasure than the dignity of human nature,"[61] Mandeville states straight away that "I believe man ... to be a compound of various passions, that all of them, as they are provoked and come uppermost, govern him by turn, whether he will or no."[62] This almost clinical attitude reminds us of his Dutch medical-school training.

Instead of stressing the uniqueness and dignity of mankind over all the other animals, Mandeville considers man to have much in common with other creatures. First in importance among these common characteristics is a natural egoism. "All untaught animals," Mandeville says, "are only solicitious of pleasing themselves, and naturally follow the bent of their own inclinations, without considering the good or harm that from their being pleased will accrue to others" (p. 40). But Mandeville's intent is not to argue just that considerations of the public good are antagonistic to man's natural desires. Among the animals man is the least capable of living together peacefully because of the great number of his appetites, which draw him into conflict with others of his kind. Not only is man an animal, but, it seems, the most contentious animal.

If the natural instincts of man are purely egoistic, how are we to explain the existence of society in which men live in relative peace? This question naturally presents itself to anyone who argues for man's unrelieved egoism. Mandeville must find an alternative to the theory of man's natural sociability that he finds in Steele and later, more explicitly, in Shaftesbury. Much of Mandeville's originality consists in the way in which he solves this problem throughout his career. The apparent virtue that we see, according to Mandeville, is the result of artifice and not nature. It resulted from the actions of politicians ambitious enough to want to rule over vast numbers of men and skillful enough to manage their vices. The politicians' chief aim has been to convince men "that it was more beneficial for everybody to conquer than to indulge his appetites, and much better to mind the public than what seemed his private interest." (p. 42).

Man is too headstrong for mere force to accomplish this transition, and there are not enough real rewards to convince man to renounce his natural inclinations. But ambitious politicians understood an ever more powerful incentive – flattery.

> They thoroughly examined all the strengths and frailities of our nature, and observing that none were either so savage as not to be charmed with praise, or so despicable as patiently to bear contempt, justly concluded that flattery must be the most powerful argument that could be used to human creatures [p. 42].

These wise men hit upon three methods for using flattery on the vanity of men. First, they extolled the nature of men above that of animals and "bestowed a thousand ecomiums on the rationality of our soul" (p. 51).

Next, they introduced honor and shame, representing one as the worst and the other as the best of the fates that could befall man. Last, they divided the entire species into two classes, the low-minded who hunted after immediate private advantage and the high-minded who were free from selfishness. Because no one would admit to being in the lower class, many pretended to have the virtue of the higher class. Though few were actually able to subdue their passions, the pride of all compelled them to "cry up self-denial and public spiritedness" (p. 45). In fact, it was the interest of the worst of them, more than any other, "to preach up public spiritedness, that they might reap the fruits of the labour and self-denial of others, and at the same time, indulge their own appetites with less disturbance . . ." (p. 48).

The "Enquiry into the Origin of Moral Virtue" is a sustained attack upon the reformers' attempt to engineer a moral revival. Mandeville argues, in a phrase that will be hurled back at him by critic after critic, that "moral virtues are the political offspring which flattery begot upon pride" (p. 51). The cries for public-spiritedness, this essay implies, were from men who had learned to pursue their own pleasures with circumspection, and who preached self-denial and virtue in order to gain control over others.

Mandeville's interest in the reforming spirit continued into the 1720s when he published, in the 1724 edition of the *Fable*, an essay on charity and Charity Schools. In the period around 1702 the emphasis of the reform movement began to shift from the enforcement of the laws through the use of informers to the establishment of schools for the sons and daughters of the poor. Disappointment over the difficulty of reforming the present generation led to the position that energy would be better spent working on the young to ensure the virtue of the next generation. Because the schools were originally less controversial than the use of informers, and through the support of the Society for Promoting Christian Knowledge, the Charity School movement gained an enthusiastic following.

The Charity Schools drew strength, as did the entire reform movement, from the fears of the propertied classes that an idle, undisciplined lower class would be a drain on the economic resources of the country and susceptible to Jacobite rebellion.[63] The goals of these schools followed from these fears. Thus Isaac Watts, for example, saw the purpose of a Charity School education to "teach the duties of humility and submission to superiors," which we might understand as a tonic against rebellion, and "diligence and industry in their business," which would ensure their economic contribution to society.[64] The education in the schools consisted of religious subjects, which emphasized the Christian virtue of humility, and the teaching of those simple tasks that would qualify the girls to be maids and the boys servants or apprentices. As Mary G. Jones states in her excellent study, "The Charity

Schools came into being chiefly, although by no means exclusively . . . to condition the children for their primary duty in life as hewers of wood and drawers of water."[65]

The first Charity School seems to have been set up in 1685 as an Anglican response to a free school that was started by Catholics in that same year. Not surprisingly, some dissenters quickly followed and set up a school of their own in Southwark. By 1704 there were 54 Charity Schools within ten miles of London and Westminster, with thirty-four more throughout the country; in 1709 the area near London boasted eighty-eight schools teaching 3,402 children; and by 1725 there were 1,417 schools in England with an enrollment of 27,703.[66] The enthusiasm for the schools and their association with the movement to reform manners can be seen in Joseph Addison's comment: "I have always looked on this institution of Charity Schools, which of late has so universally prevailed throughout the whole nation, as the glory of the age we live in, and the most proper means that can be made use of to recover it out of its present degeneracy and depravation of manners."[67] Richard Steele voiced similar sentiments in the *Spectator*: "The Charity Schools, which have been erected of late years, are the greatest instance of public spirit the age has produced."[68]

Mandeville's attack on the Charity Schools begins with an analysis of the virtue of charity. He defines it rigorously as "that virtue by which part of that sincere love we have for our selves is transferred pure and unmixed to others, not tied to us by the bonds of friendship and consanguinity . . . ."[69] This definition immediately rules out the favours we might do for our relations because, says Mandeville, we are expected under the rules of honor to care for our own. The strict definition demands that charitable acts be done solely because of our love for others. Any action that is tainted by self-love, as in the concern for one's own reputation, can have no claim to the virtue of charity.

Mandeville seeks to limit further the domain of charitable acts by distinguishing between charity and pity or compassion. Pity is an innate passion that makes "so forcible an impression upon us, as to make us uneasy" (p. 254). Actions performed through pity, because they have as their object the elimination of uneasiness in the actor, and are therefore self-interested, cannot be considered a virtue. These strict criteria for the performance of a virtuous act admirably serve Mandeville's purpose by making it less difficult to show that underneath apparently charitable acts are considerations of self-interest.

If charity is not the cause for the rapid increase in the Charity Schools, what is? Mandeville sees two general causes. The first can be found in a universal human attribute:

> One motive above all, which is none of the least with the most of them, is to be carefully concealed. I mean the satisfaction there is in

ordering and directing. There is a melodious sound in the word governor that is charming to mean people . . . . there is a pleasure in ruling over anything, and it is this chiefly that supports human nature in the tedious slavery of school masters [p. 280].

The second concerns the specific political situation in England in the first part of the eighteenth century. In the period after 1710 when the Tories came to power, the Charity Schools were the objects of considerable party rivalry. Mandeville attributes part of the enthusiasm for the schools "to the rigid party-men that are zealous for their cause" (p. 277). This opinion is substantiated by Mary Jones. She notes: "It was the unhappy fate of the English Charity Schools to act as pawns in the game of party politics between high and low churchmen in the first quarter of the eighteenth century."[70] Between 1710 and 1716 there was a concerted effort on the part of the Tories to gain control over the schools. It seems that they were successful in inserting Jacobite masters and teachings into many of the schools in London. After 1716 the low churchmen began to counterattack, but the schools were thereafter associated with the high-church party.[71]

The primary line of attack, however, concerned the economic consequences that Mandeville foresaw resulting from the widespread popularity of charity schools. Briefly, Mandeville's ideas can be summarized this way.[72] The economic well-being of the nation depends upon the presence of a large number of men who are content to labor hard all day long. Because men are naturally lazy they will not work unless forced by necessity to do so. The education of the poor threatens to rob the nation of their productivity. First, the time children are in school could be spent working; second, the education the poor children receive, will make them lazy and indolent; they will look with contempt upon hard labor.

It is possible to see hints of these ideas as early as the *Female Tatler*. The notion that workers are best kept in ignorance for their own good and society's can be seen in this statement:

Were not industry and stupidity a better composition for a tyler, than knowledge and curiosity. Tis true, indeed, by the help of letters he may find a way to excuse his neglects and mistakes, but tis certain our homes would be more secured from raining in, by the man that knew nothing of the matter.[73]

The acquisition of knowledge will not affect the virtue of a poor child. His character is molded by his family, and his law-abidingness determined by the rigor of the laws. Education can only make a poor child clever, accustom him to idleness, and make him unhappy with his proper station.

Two small pamphlets published by Mandeville in the 1720s were also directed specifically against the reform movement. In *A Modest Defense of Publick Stews* (1724), Mandeville argued against the reformers' attempts to suppress lewdness. Lust, he argued, must have an outlet, and to that end, he proposed that the government establish legal brothels. Such houses would take many disorderly people off the street and bring them under government control, they would help control disease, and they would bring an end to the killing of unwanted children. Mandeville objected to this last practice because it held down the population and impaired the productive capacity of England. His concern for a stable class structure can be seen in the rather peculiar argument that the brothels would provide a way for young men of rank to gain experience so that they would not marry the first young lady, whatever her social position, with whom they fell in love.

In *An Enquiry into the Causes of the Frequent Executions at Tyburn* (1725), Mandeville addressed the problem of crime. He disagreed with the attempts to control crime through reforming manners, or educating children in charity schools. Instead, he concentrated on suggesting new laws and penalties, the most specific of which was a procedure for hanging that he thought would help deter crime.

Throughout Mandeville's opposition to the Societies for the Reformation of Manners as seen in *Typhon, The Grumbling Hive*, the *Female Tatler*, the "Enquiry into the Origin of Virtue," the "Essay on Charity and Charity Schools," *A Modest Defense of Public Stews* and *An Enquiry into the Causes of the Frequent Executions of Tyburn*, one can discern certain major themes. Behind the calls for a moral reformation Mandeville uncovered pride, hypocrisy, and self-interest. He dissented from that most characteristic canon of social thought of the period that virtue constitutes the cement that holds society together. His examination of society revealed the unimportance of virtue, and put in its place passions, needs, and self-interests. Since we cannot call these virtues, we must admit that a complex society demands that vice be mixed with virtue.

The delusions of the moralists would be less important were it not for the tendency of their programs to disrupt economic prosperity. Never far below the surface of Mandeville's moral concerns are his economic interests. The reformers' refusal to acknowledge the role of vanity, pride, and luxury could adversely affect the spending habits of the upper classes. At the same time, the attempt to educate the lower classes could deprive the country of the laboring poor. In both cases the moralists who enjoyed the fruits of English prosperity would find that they had eliminated the conditions which made it possible.

# Chapter 2 Mandeville and the French Moral Tradition

Although Mandeville's views differed widely from those of his contemporaries and found few, if any, followers, he was not simply an eccentric who surfaced unaccountably. His thought reflected the confluence of some important trends in the intellectual and economic development of the late seventeenth and early eighteenth centuries. This chapter will consider the French intellectual tradition, which drew a great deal of its strength from the religious thought of the Jansenists and which was carried on to the end of the seventeenth century by men such as La Rochefoucauld, Jacques Esprit, and La Fontaine, who were sympathetic to Jansenism.[1] Closely associated with this religious sentiment was a tradition of skepticism, influenced by Montaigne,[2] which reached its apex in this period in the thought of Pierre Bayle. Both Jansenist fideism and skepticism begin with an awareness of the weakness of reason, the strength of the passions, and particularly the power of pride and vanity; and both stress the unmasking of supposedly virtuous activity and the reduction of that activity to the working of self-love. Fideism, of course, transcends the contradictions of this world by a leap of faith, while a nonreligious skepticism remains tied to the world.

Mandeville's association with the French intellectual tradition was not lost on his contemporaries. Almost all of those who noted Mandeville's intellectual origins noted the importance of Bayle, while many also mentioned Esprit and La Rochefoucauld.[3] Nor was it lost on those men who were part of the movement for the reformation of manners that the French moral tradition was antagonistic to their own. Bickerstaff, after having expounded on his ambition to raise the "grandeur of the soul," remarked:

> I could never read any of our modish French authors . . . without being for some time out of humour with myself . . . . Their business is, to depreciate human nature, and consider it under its worst appearances. They give mean interpretations and base motives to

the worthiest actions: they resolve virtue and vice into constitution. In short, they endeavor to make no distinction between man and man, or between the species of man and that of brutes. As an instance of this kind of author, among many others, let us examine the celebrated Rochefoucauld, who is the great philosopher for administering of consolation to the idle, the envious, and worthless part of mankind.[4]

The origins of Jansenism can be traced to Cornelis Jansen's education at the University of Louvain and his decision there to join the camp of those who defended Michael du Bay, who had been a professor at Louvain. This decision irrevocably put Jansen in opposition to the powerful Society of Jesus. The controversy initiated by Bay centered on the doctrines of grace and original sin. Bay used the writings of St. Augustine against the Pelagians to stress, in short, the depravity of man after original sin, the belief that all sins deserve eternal punishment, that there was no such thing as natural virtue, and that charity like all other virtues was a transitory impulse received from God. Bay's method was also important. He set up the anti-Pelagian writings of St. Augustine as the authoritative teachings on grace. Furthermore, he rejected the glosses of the Scholastics on Augustine and reveled in reaching conclusions different from theirs.[5]

In the early seventeenth century Jansen, under the influence of Bay's ideas, undertook with the abbot Saint-Cyran an exchange of ideas on the possible reform of the Catholic Church. Like Bay, Jansen took as his inspiration the writings of St. Augustine. In 1640, two years after his death, the great work of Cornelis Jansen, the *Augustinus*, was published. The central doctrine of Jansen and Jansenism was that of efficacious grace, which the Jansenists opposed to the Jesuit doctrine of sufficient grace. Simply put, in the Jesuit doctrine, "It is claimed that sufficient grace for salvation is never denied to man, and that the factual efficacity of grace depends upon free human consent, although its infallibility depends upon God, the mode of whose prescience includes and transcends human indetermination."[6] The key element in their doctrine was that man had a role in and was capable of saving himself. Against this the Jansenists argued that "the salvation of man after the sin of Adam and the fall could come only as a free gift of God and not from human effort, which could no more win grace by itself than it could resist it."[7]

The doctrines of Jansenism were directed specifically at the "devout humanism" of the Jesuits. The more optimistic theology of the Jesuits sought to reconcile the impulses of natural man with the requirements of religion. This attitude can be seen in their apologies, for example, for the desire for reputation and glory. In this view the desire for earthly glory was the "confused consciousness of the soul's immortal destiny"

(p. 91). The thrust of the neo-Scholasticism of the Jesuits, ultimately based on the writings of Aquinas, was to tie the natural to the divine by an unbroken rising scale of perfections, and thus to save the natural.

This theological stance was especially favorable to the outlook of a self-confident aristocracy. It was consistent with their high self-esteem and their concern with pride and glory. As Paul Benichou points out, "moral optimism is still feeling the effects of its aristocratic origins; this projection of the ego into the realm of greatness is above all a trait of the aristocracy" (p. 79).

Jansenism, according to Lucien Goldmann,[8] rose to importance during the middle years of the seventeenth century when the position of a part of the aristocracy and upper bourgeoisie was deteriorating. These were the years of the greatest growth of the royal bureaucracy and of the failure in the 1650s of the aristocratic revolt known as the Fronde. Jansenism, Goldmann maintains, was the expression of those who wanted to withdraw from the world in the face of the declining position of their class. Their pessimistic theological ideas, which stressed the depravity of all men after the fall, the impotence of men to effect their own salvation, the enormous separation between man and God, and the unregenerate evil of nature, expressed the unfavorable situation in which this group found itself. Jansenists condemned the state of morality which surrounded them and championed the most rigorous moral rules, though without any real hope that they could ever be obeyed completely. In order to defend their pessimistic view, the Jansenists engaged in a most subtle psychological analysis, penetrating the unconscious desires of men and exposing beneath even the most sublime actions the operation of the appetites and self-love. The "recourse to the unconscious elements in men is . . . their [Jansenists'] most powerful weapon when they want to challenge the assertions of idealism."[9]

In Blaise Pascal we see the finest expression of the Jansenist religious outlook. It starts from the destruction of all the levels that in neo-Scholastic thought mediate between man and God. What remains is the "wretchedness of man without God" or the "happiness of man with God," corrupt nature or the Redeemer.[10] Fallen man is incapable of bridging the void between himself and God by his reason or any of his actions. He is incapable of either proving that God exists or knowing His nature. "If there is a God, he is infinitely beyond our comprehension, since being indivisible and without limits, he bears no relation to us. We are therefore incapable of knowing either what he is or whether he is" (p. 150). But the heart tells man what reason is incapable of knowing. If it tells man God exists, he must wager it is so.

The awareness of the "infinite chasm" that separates man from God is based not only on the awareness of His greatness, but also on the most rigorous understanding of mankind's original sin. Man withdrew from the rule of God and "wanted to make himself his own center . . . setting himself up as [God's] equal" (p. 77). Man centers all things in himself, distorting his reason and his passions. He seems incapable even of understanding his own nature. "We are nothing but lies, duplicity, contradiction, and we hide and disguise ourselves from ourselves (p. 240). Even those actions which seem virtuous have their roots in selfishness. Pity for the unfortunate, for example, is displayed only "to win a reputation for sympathy without giving anything in return" (p. 240). If reputation is not the reason for good actions, our virtues may be merely "the counter balance of two opposing vices" (p. 242), so that if one vice were taken away we would fall into the other.

In Jacques Esprit, often mentioned by contemporaries as a possible influence on Mandeville, we see similiar ideas motivated by a devout religious belief. While most men believe that "actions which seem reasonable, just, good, and generous, proceed from reason, justice, goodness and generosity," Esprit thinks this is an "erroneous opinion."[11] The "hidden causes of human action" are found in "self love . . . the master and tyrant of man."[12] All men, perhaps especially philosophers, are governed by interest. The Stoic philosophers, always targets of Jansenist thought, made an ideal of moral good only because they loved the glory and esteem that attended good acts. Moreover, these were ambitious men who taught others to despise wealth so that they might be thought more important than those who had wealth and esteem. The celebrated desire for the truth in these philosophers most probably had its roots in mere curiosity, a disposition to find fault in others, a prideful attempt to increase their own value through the acquisition of knowledge, or through the self-love that compelled them to prove a point merely because it was their own.[13]

Mandeville's work clearly shows certain similarities with this kind of religious thought. Mandeville maintains throughout his work a rigorous moral standard, which man is unable to live up to because of his inability to act except from self-love. In Jansenism and Mandeville's thought a psychological analysis is used to unmask (a motif common to both) the working of self-love even in seemingly virtuous activity. Individuals who proclaimed a  mystical union with God or who argued for a renewed moral awareness to serve as the basis of an earthly community with any hope of success would be treated skeptically by either. In both the Jansensists' and Mandeville's thought. God has been hidden from man.

It is interesting to consider the effects of this attitude on social analysis. This view of human nature makes it impossible to believe that society coheres because of man's natural sociableness or his ability to act according to moral rules. If man's actions are all traceable to self-love then the key to the forces that hold society together must be found there. In the Jansenist Pierre Nicole we find this idea explicitly stated. He wrote that "self love drove men from intolerable anarchy into society; it is the first principle of human behaviour and the foundation of civil law . . . . utility is the exclusive criterion, the unique source from which the canons of human behavior are derived."[14] In another work he stated this idea even more clearly: "enlightened self love will be able to correct all the outward faults of the world, and to form a well regulated society."[15] It was popular in the last half of the seventeenth century to look to pride, vanity, and the universal desire for esteem as the means by which self-love enabled men to accommodate themselves to others.[16] Nicole further suggested that self-interest worked through trade to link men together. It is this aspect of Jansenism – its refusal to see virtue as the cement holding society together – which constitutes its contribution to social thought and which is most important to the consideration of the tradition out of which Mandeville emerged.[17]

There is, however, one absolutely central aspect of Jansenism that is not found in Mandeville. Goldmann points out that devoutly religious Jansenism constitutes one of the great tragic visions of man's condition. The Jansenist is defined by two paradoxical elements in his thought. He is both extremely realistic about the fallen nature of man and the nature of his social existence, while at the same time he demands the fulfillment of absolute religious values. As Goldmann says, "The greatness of tragic man lies in the fact that he sees and recognizes these opposite and inimical elements in the clear light of absolute truth, and yet never accepts that this shall be so. For if he were to accept them, he would destroy the paradox, he would give up his greatness and make do with his poverty and wretchedness."[18] In fact, this is precisely what Mandeville has done. He uses and perhaps even believes in the rigorous definition of morality, but he has given up the demand that it be achieved. He is willing to make do with, accept fully, man in his fallen state. The tragedy that is central to Jansenism cannot be found in Mandeville.

La Rochefoucauld is probably the most well known of the French *moralistes* who wrote in the second half of the seventeenth century and who helped to carry on the Jansenist tradition. The *moraliste* was "not concerned with ethical issues only but with a picture of human behaviour which shall throw into relief its paradox, its complexity, in a word which shall suggest the irony of the human condition."[19] La Rochefoucauld was a close friend of Jacques Esprit, he was sympathetic to Jansenism, and was part of the same salon frequented by La Fontaine. Salon society was based on a leisured class which, since the Fronde, was barred from public life. Cut off from military or political topics, which were often too dangerous to discuss, and, under the influence of Jansenist ideas, salon society probed the private world of the motivations and reactions of mankind.[20] Its aim was to see behind the public appearance, which seemed to be mere illusion, and to penetrate to the actual springs of action.

When La Rochefoucauld takes off the mask that men wear in public he does not find that reason or virtue plays an important role in men's actions. Instead he finds that "In the human heart there is an endless procreation of passions: as soon as one is dethroned, another almost always comes to power."[21] The object of these passions is rarely the welfare of other men. To the contrary, "We can love nothing," he says, "except as it concerns us personally . . ." (No. 81). The Stoicism that was popular in the first part of the century in France was subjected to a withering attack by the *moralistes* in the second half of the century. In the place of a rational man in control of his passions La Rochefoucauld and others substitute a man dominated by passions that are untouched by the reason, now seen as impotent. "The mind," La Rochefoucauld contends, "is always the dupe of the heart" (No. 102).

The general vision stressing the limitations of reason is buttressed by the reduction of apparent virtues to the effects of mere passions. With regard to the ideal of moderation and the golden mean, he states: "We have made a virtue of moderation that we may limit the ambitions of the great and may console the mediocre for their want of fortune or ability" (No. 308). Moderation means only "weakness and laziness of spirit" (No. 293). Courage fares no better, since it results from "the love of glory, the fear of disgrace, and incentive to succeed, the desire to live in comfort, and the instinct to humiliate others . . ." (No. 213). As a final example of La Rochefoucauld's penetration into the human heart, consider what some have thought to be the greatest pleasure of men – friendship. La Rochefoucauld uncovers selfishness even there. "What men call friendship is just an arrangement for mutual gain and an exchange of favors: in short, a business where self interest always sets out to obtain something" (No. 83).

The reduction of virtues to amoral or vicious passions means conversely that characteristics normally thought of as vicious can lead to virtuous actions, at least in terms of public appearance. This realization is an important part of the attempt by the *moralistes* to show the world in all its complexity and paradox. The idea that "passions often beget their opposites" (No. 11), part of the complexity La Rochefoucauld sees, can be traced to the fact that "self interest speaks all sorts of languages and plays all sorts of roles, even that of disinterestedness" (No. 39). Thus, in the same way that poisons, properly mixed, can help make up medicine, the vices of men can help make up their virtues (No. 183; see also No. 519).

Throughout La Rochefoucauld we find considerable attention given to the manifestation of self-love in the form of desiring and finding a special satisfaction in the praise of others. He writes: "Pride exists equally in all men; the only difference lies in what ways they manifest it" (No. 35). Many of the manifestations of pride are in the form of acts that appear virtuous. Our desire to be praised "strengthens our powers of virtue" (No. 50; see also No. 598). Pride can lead to kindness when we confront the mistakes of others (No. 37), and "except for their enormous vanity, heroes are like the rest of us" (No. 24). In all these cases pride and vanity compel us to wear a mask in public, to perform in acceptable ways and pretend we are something we are not. But this is not the end of pride's work. The illusion that we perform good acts for others is often finally believed ourselves. Cruelly La Rochefoucauld reminds us that "However well people speak of us, they teach us nothing new" (No. 303). We are "so much in the habit of wearing a disguise before others that we finally appear disguised before ourselves" (No. 119).

La Rochefoucauld serves to show how many of the specific psychological insights we see in Mandeville can be found in the *moralistes* of late seventeeth-century France. Charity, pity, moderation, courage, honor are all reduced by La Rochefoucauld to different manifestations of self-love. Like all the Jansenists before him, he stresses the weaknesses and limitations of man's ability to reason. Moreover, the forces of self-love and pride coupled with the weakness of reason result in man even deluding himself. The ideal of an *honnête homme*, a man not deluded by pride, who has achieved a harmony between private motive and public performance, seems impossible to reach. But because the ideal is seriously maintained the tragedy of man remains. "To punish man for original sin, God has let him deify his love of self, that he may be tortured by it at every stage of life" (No. 509).

These quotations specifically illustrate the difference between Mandeville and the earlier part of the tradition out of which he emerged. La Rochefoucauld found his inspiration in the actions of the court and a defeated aristocracy. His interest was primarily with the complexity of individual life and the transformation of vice into virtue within each man. There was little interest in social life and virtually no interest in economic affairs. In short, the difference between La Rochefoucauld and Mandeville is the difference between a disappointed French aristocrat in the seventeenth century and a more confident, if satirical, Dutch or English bourgeois.

Mandeville's ties to the French *moralistes* of the late seventeenth century can be seen clearly and directly through his interest in that "Great Man in France, Monsieur de la Fontaine."[22] La Fontaine was a member of the same salon at Mme de Lafayette's as La Rochefoucauld. Influenced, like so many others in this period, by Jansenist ideas, he saw himself attacking what he thought was the Stoic belief in extirpating all desires and passions. But less rigorous than more religious Jansenists, he thought life was to be enjoyed. The best means to accomplish this task was through contentment, limited ambitions, moderation, and self-knowledge. Pride, the passion that inhibits this moderation most by deluding man about his powers and ruining his contentment, is criticized most severely.

Mandeville's translation of the *fables* of La Fontaine published in 1703, entitled *Some Fables after the Easie and Familiar Method of Monsieur de la Fontaine*, was probably Mandeville's first published work in English. In 1704 additional fables were added and published as *Aesop Dress'd*, which was the first book-length translation of La Fontaine's fables into English. In this collection Mandeville also added two of his own verses – "The Carp" and "The Nightingale and the Owl."

These fables were translated by Mandeville during a period in which many Englishmen were concerned with the reformation of manners and just two years before Mandeville's attack on that movement in *The Grumbling Hive*. We are able to see in them certain themes from the tradition of the *moralistes*, which will be used by Mandeville in his criticism of public-spiritedness. The frank acceptance of many of the vices and passions of man, the foolishness involved in refusing to accept one's life, and the self-deluding effects of pride are the main themes in these fables.

The strength of the passions and mankind's inability to control them, one of the dominant themes of Jansenism, can be found throughout the satirical fables of La Fontaine. The "Drunkard and His Wife," for example, begins "Man is so obstinate a creature / No remedy can change his nature / Fear, shame, all ineffectual prove / to cure us from the vice we love" (p. 24). The strength of a particular passion, love, is seen in the moral to another fable, in which La Fontaine writes: "Where love his tyranny commences; / There, farewell prudence, farewell senses" (p. 43).

The passion that is most destructive and in which La Fontaine and Mandeville seem most interested is pride. In one of the first fables in the collection, an ambitious frog tries to become as large as an ox by puffing himself up. His only reward is to end by bursting (pp. 4–5). Similarly, in "The Lyon and the Gnat," a gnat, after he had successfully conquered a lion, "Puffed up and blinded with his glory, / He met a cobweb in his way, / And fell a silly spider's prey" (pp. 49–50).

In both fables Mandeville has added lines to the original, which makes the effect of pride more explicit. In "The Lyon and the Gnat" the line "Puffed up and blinded with his glory" is Mandeville's own. In "The Frog" he adds these lines, which relate pride more directly to early eighteenth-century England.

So full of pride is every age!
A citizen must have a page,
A petty prince ambassadors,
And tradesmens children governors;

A fellow, that isn't worth a louse,
Still keeps his coach and country house
A merchant swelled with haughtiness,
Looks ten times bigger than he is . . . [p. 5].

The two fables that Mandeville wrote for the *Aesop Dress'd* collection also have as their subject pride. "The Carp" satirizes the grand tour of Europe as a proper education. Mandeville's moral is:

Some fops that visit France and Rome,
Before they know what's done at home
Look like our carp when come again.
Strange countries may improve a man,
That knew the world before he went;
But he that sets out ignorant,
When only vanity intices,
Brings nothing from 'em, but their vices [p. 27].

The other original fable of Mandeville's, "The Nightingale and the Owl," tells the story of the evil consequences that are visited upon a prideful nightingale and the successes of a humble owl (p. 27).

Pride deludes a man into underestimating his own limitations. It deludes him into imagining that his powers are greater than they are, that he deserves a much better situation than he has, and that his knowledge is so great that he could properly order the world around him. If man acts upon his prideful view of the world, the results are usually disaster. In "The Milk Woman" a "strapping dame" carrying milk to sell in town dreams of the money she will receive, and concocts a chain of events that will make her rich, only to spill the milk in the process. In another fable, a country bumpkin cannot understand why the mighty oak carries small acorns instead of using its size to support pumpkins, until one day sitting under an oak tree an acorn falls on his head and he is able to imagine what would have happened if it had been a pumpkin instead. The moral, which was added by Mandeville, states:

The world's vast fabrick is so well
contrived by its Creator's skill,
There's nothing in it, but what is good
To him, by whom it's understood;
And what opposes human sense,
Shows but pride and ignorance [p. 7].

In another fable the hands and feet decide to revolt against the belly, who, they think, is enjoying itself while they labor. After the hands and feet go on strike; it is too late for them to realize "how he, / whom they accused of gluttony, of laziness, ingratitude, / Had labored for the common good, / by ways they never understood" (p. 9). The last example, "The Frogs Asking for a King," foreshadows a device Mandeville will use in *The Grumbling Hive*. Unsatisfied frogs ask Jove to send them a king. But soon dissatisfied with the one they are sent (a log) because he is too quiet, they ask for a livelier king. Jove, angered by their refusal to be content, sends them a crane who proceeds to devour the frog community.

In these fables of La Fontaine's we see certain themes that Mandeville will find useful in his satirical attack on the movement to reform manners. Perhaps the translation itself is part of Mandeville's opposition to this group. That Mandeville saw the relevance of the fables seems clear, given that later editions of the *Female Tatler*, which, as I have tried to show, were directed against the reform movement, carried his fable "The Carp" as well as two of the La Fontaine fables in translation.[23] The message of these fables, which are concerned with pride, also seems clear. Attempts to initiate large-scale reform of society are the result of pride, which causes man to overstate his own knowledge and abilities. Most men do not understand the mechanisms by which society coheres. This theme is found throughout Mandeville, it is his main accusation against the Societies for the Reformation of Manners, and it is present in his earliest work – the translation of La Fontaine.

La Rochefoucauld provides an excellent example of the style and climate of opinion found in the "classical period" of French literature with which Mandeville must have been familiar. Through Mandeville's translation of La Fontaine's fables we can see his direct interest in this tradition. But the most important Frenchman to influence Mandeville's thought was Pierre Bayle. Mandeville recognizes his debt to Bayle in *Free Thoughts* when he says: "Those who are versed in books will soon discover, that I have made great use of Monsieur Baile . . . ."[24] Bayle, it is interesting to note, was giving public lectures in Rotterdam at the same time Mandeville was attending school in that city, though there is no evidence that Mandeville attended Bayle's lectures. It is not surprising to find that some reformers viewed Bayle in the same way that Steele saw La Rochefoucauld. In one periodical associated with the reform movement the authors refer to Bayle's "pernicious, abominable notions . . . [and] . . . all his prophane, irreligious paradoxes and whimsies."[25]

After Bayle was forced to leave France because of his Protestant religion, and after his brother had died from being imprisoned for religious reasons, he devoted his new life in Holland to attacking orthodoxy and defending toleration. He argued not only against all attempts to base orthodoxy on the miraculous, but also against the efforts to use reason to find the one correct position. "Now in our present condition it is impossible for us to know with certainty that that which appears to us to be true is in fact the absolute truth."[26] Throughout his greatest work, *The Historical and Critical Dictionary*, he subjects religious ideas to a withering attack. His comments on Socinians, Manicheans, and numerous religious sects are all made to show that "our reason serves only to confound everything, and makes us doubt of everything."[27]

The logical analysis Bayle uses to discredit all attempts to build absolute truth upon reason is less important for this study than his method, used most effectively in the *Miscellaneous Reflections on the Comet. . .*, of subjecting the ideals of rationalist Christianity to psychological analysis. Whether as a ploy or as the result of sincere piety, he makes his task easier by adopting an extremely rigorous, rationalist notion of virtue. A Christian, he declares, must be able "to mortify his lusts, to love his enemies, to bear injuries and contempt with cheerfulness; in a word, to strive against the torrent of sensual inclination."[28] Throughout Bayle's work true virtue is identified with following the principles of abstract reason or rigorous religious standards.

In the section of the *Miscellaneous Reflections* that considers a society of atheists, Bayle tries to show how little his conception of virtue is adhered to among religious Europeans, by comparing them to men who have no religion at all. "What induces us to believe Atheism the most fearful state, is only a common prejudice concerning the dictates of conscience, taken to be the rule of human actions, merely for want of examining their true springs."[29] Like so many other French writers of the period, he maintains that the real motivations of men, atheist or religious, are "the present reigning passion of his heart . . . the natural inclination for pleasure."[30] Behind all individual passions and pleasures we find "that inseparable passion of our nature"[31] self-love. Men relish all things that flatter their vanity and gratify their lust. But most of all self-love "carrys us to pant ardently after riches, as the source of all these advantages."[32]

This passage is especially interesting because of the importance it gives to avarice. In La Rochefoucauld and La Fontaine it was always clear that we were in the world of the aristocracy and the court. The vision that we encounter through these two writers seems to mirror the life of a courtier. While this vision continues in Bayle (so that our awareness of lust is undiminished), we are at the same time more aware of avarice as a vice and of the life of the merchant.[33]

It seems inevitable that writers who hold both a strict view of virtue and a pessimistic view of man's nature will end by acknowledging that vices have as much to do with the continuation of social life as virtues. We saw this paradox in the Jansenists, in La Rochefoucauld, and now we see it in Bayle. His effort to demonstrate that a society of atheists would act no differently from a society of Christians must rest on show-

ing that what order and semblance of virtue exist in the Christian society come from the passions and self-love. Thus,

> . . . an inclination to pity, sobriety, good nature arises not from the
> supposition of a god . . . but from the particular natural temper and
> constitution, fortified by education, by self love, vain glory, an in-
> stinct of reason, or such like motives, which prevail in atheists as well
> as others.[34]

Like others in this period, Bayle lays special stress on vanity and
pride. Bayle's low opinion of women helps explain why the chastity of
women is one of his favorite examples of the way in which pride works.
"Since religion is incapable of subduing the inclination of nature,"[35]
Bayle finds the motivation for chastity elsewhere. "If they who have
carried this duty to the rigor, examine themselves, they will find . . .
that the thought of what will the world say has conduced to it, more
than any other motive . . . loss of honor is all they dread."[36] A few
pages later Bayle uses the example of giving alms to the poor as another
instance of the desire for good reputation motivating seemingly virtuous
actions. The Jansenist Nicole had also written that charity and self-love
often had the same consequences.

However, Bayle takes a step which separates his paradox from those
before. He not only suggests that vices can motivate the same acts as
virtues; he goes so far as to say that if a society wants to prosper, it must
rely exclusively on vices. A country made up of men who acted sincerely
on Christian precepts could not last.

> The true Christians, it seems to me, consider themselves as voyagers
> and pilgrims who are traveling to heaven, their true country. They
> regard the world as a banishment . . . . they are . . . always attentive
> to mortify their flesh, to repress the love of riches and of honors, to
> repress the pleasures of the flesh, and to subdue . . . pride . . . .
> Examine this thing well and you will find, I am certain, that a
> nation totally composed of people like that would be soon enslaved if
> an enemy undertook to conquer it, because they would be unable to
> furnish themselves with good soldiers, or enough money to pay the
> expenses of soldiers.[37]

A nation that exists in a world filled with foreign enemies can keep
Christian doctrines only in theory. In practice it must live according to
the laws of nature, which allow it to fight back. His advice to countries
that desire wealth and power is straightforward.

> Maintain avarice and ambition in all their ardor, prohibit them only
> in theft and fraud, animate them in all other respects by rewards:
> promote pensions for those who invent new manufactures, or new
> means of increasing commerce . . . . Do not fear the effects of the love

of gold: it is truly a poison which results in a thousand corrupt passions, and which excites and ferments the corruptions of the heart. It is this that caused the most pernicious disorders of the Roman Republic .... But do not be concerned, it is not necessary that the same things happen in all centuries and in all kinds of climate .... You know the maxim that a dishonest man is able to be a good citizen. He renders services that an honest man is incapable of rendering.[38]

While Bayle has gone a long way to placing the mechanism for society's operation in selfish passions, he has not overlooked the importance of government and laws. "Very severe laws ... very well executed"[39] would be required in a commonwealth of pagans and atheists just as they are required in our own. It would be a mistake to imagine that the awareness in these writers of the importance of self-interest in ordering society is tantamount to the laissez-faire doctrine of a self-regulating society. The effect of Jansenism and the skepticism of this period is in precisely the opposite direction.[40] Bayle's emphasis on the necessity of laws and government, for example, enables Lionel Rothkrug to characterize him as a mercantilist.[41]

The doctrine that fallen man has been given a reprieve, a mechanism in his depraved nature which enables him to reach a semblance of virtue, has undergone a considerable change from La Rochefoucauld to Bayle. Originally, the fact that fallen men were able to live in society merely showed that pride or *amour-propre* could act as a substitute for virtue. At this point, the emphasis was upon the foibles of individual men and the ways in which the self-interested passions within the individual could motivate him to act correctly. In Bayle this position has changed. He shows that Christian virtues are incompatible with the world of power and wealth. The passions do not substitute for Christian virtues, but actually replace them. Moreover, the emphasis is now upon the effects of the passions in society as much as in the individual. The idea that there are two kinds of societies, one virtuous, small, and unconcerned with the world, the other powerful, rich, and full of vice, will be found again in Mandeville, who like Bayle will opt for the second kind of society, and, for instance, in Rousseau who will seek to reconstruct the first. The vision of Bayle and Mandeville is essentially the mercantilist vision, which desires wealth and power, and understands that it must not only tolerate, but also embrace many actions that are vicious by standard Christian ideals.

Mandeville's opposition to the reformation of manners stems from his belief that the virtue and public-spiritedness they demand are not only a sham, but also positively incompatible with a wealthy and powerful England. These lessons he learned from men like Nicole, La Rochefoucauld, La Fontaine, and, most of all, Pierre Bayle.

# Chapter 3 Mandeville and Shaftesbury

The sharp distinction found in Jansenist thought between the "hidden God" and natural man was consistent with the skeptical tradition that led Bayle to show that Christian virtues were incompatible with a prosperous state. Mandeville took this division and made it the center of his thought.

> Would you render a society of men strong and powerful, you must touch their passions. Divide the land, tho' there be never so much to spare, and their possessions will make them covetous: rouse them, tho' but in jest, from their idleness with praises, and pride will set them to work in earnest: teach them trades and handicrafts, and you'll bring envy and emulation among them: To increase their numbers, set up a variety of manufactures, and leave no ground uncultivated .... Would you have them bold and warlike, turn to military discipline, make good use of their fear, and flatter their vanity with art and assiduity: but would you moreover render them an opulent, knowing and polite nation, teach 'em commerce with foreign countries, and if possible get into the sea, which to compass spare no labour nor industry, and let no difficulty deter you from it ... encourage trade in every branch of it; this will bring riches, and where they are, arts and science will soon follow ....
>
> But would you have a frugal and honest society, the best policy is to preserve men in their native simplicity, strive not to increase their numbers; let them never be acquainted with strangers or superfluities, but remove and keep from them every thing that might raise their desires, or improve their understanding.
>
> Great wealth and foreign treasure will ever scorn to come among men, unless you'll admit their inseparable companions, avarice and luxury: Where trade is considerable fraud will intrude. To be at once well-bred and sincere, is no less than a contradiction; and therefore while man advances in knowledge and his manners are polish'd, we must expect to see at the same time his desires enlarg'd, his appetites refin'd, and his vices increas'd.[1]

Mandeville has postulated two alternative courses of life for men – altruistic virtue or worldly prosperity. His insistence upon the incompatibility of these alternatives, based on a proper understanding of the different principles that characterize each, constituted the basis of his arguments with the moralists found in early eighteenth-century England. It was because he posed the conflict between virtue and commerce so starkly that he also had such great influence upon the most important moral philosophers of the later part of the century – Hutcheson, Hume, and Smith – all of whom had to rejoin what Mandeville had torn asunder.

Mandeville developed his moral psychology, the basis of the principles that separate virtue and commerce, in opposition to two groups of writers. The first group we have already encountered in the movement to reform manners. This group generally represented the traditional Christian moral perspective. There was, however, another target of Mandeville's satire – Anthony Ashley Cooper III, Lord Shaftesbury. Mandeville's awareness of and opposition to Shaftesbury can be seen in the opening to "A Search into the Nature of Society," which was appended to the 1723 edition of the *Fable*, vol. 1. He states:

> The attentive reader, who perused the forgoing part of the book, will soon perceive that two systems cannot be more opposite than his Lordship's and mine. His notions I confess are generous and refined: They are a high compliment to human kind . . . . what a pity it is they are not true.[2]

Though the *Characteristics* appeared in 1711, it does not seem that Shaftesbury became Mandeville's chief target until the 1720s. Like the moral reformers, Shaftesbury, according to Mandeville, misunderstood the proper mix of public concern and private interest that characterized prosperous eighteenth-century England.

Over a half century earlier Jansenism and many of those touched with Jansenist ideas led an all-out attack on aristocratic virtue and the revival of Stoicism. The exaltation of man and nature was inimical to Port-Royal. Pascal himself set out to refute the Stoic Epictetus.[3] In the early eighteenth century in England the most well-known representative of aristocratic Stoic thought was Lord Shaftesbury. It is not surprising then to see Mandeville, so heavily influenced by the French moralist tradition, criticize him.

Shaftesbury seems to have had two groups in mind when he wrote the *Characteristics*. One group comprised orthodox religious thinkers who argued that since the fall the greatest spur to virtuous action for fallen men was the reward of heaven and the punishment of hell. The second group of writers with whom he disagreed was comprised of men like Hobbes and La Rochefoucauld. They too disparaged human nature by arguing that man acted only from narrow self-interest.

Against both groups Shaftesbury wanted to defend human nature and, in a more general way, nature itself. In the realm of social thought this attempt meant defending the idea of a common good and the ability of men to act in public-spirited ways.

The injunction to follow nature so common in the contemporary world, identified with the Stoics in the ancient world and the neo-Stoics in seventeenth-century England and France, can be clearly seen in Shaftesbury.

> O glorious nature! Supremely fair, and sovereignly good! All-loving and all-lovely, all-divine . . . whose every single work affords an ampler scene, and is a nobler spectacle than all which ever art presented! O mighty nature! Wise substitute of Providence . . . I sing of nature's order in created beings, and celebrate the beautys which resolve, in thee, the source and principle of all beauty and perfection.[4]

This view of nature leads Shaftesbury, for instance, to object to the belief in miracles held by orthodox churchmen because it destroyed "that admirable simplicity of order"[5] which he finds in nature. His view of nature demands that he find even more objectionable the position he associates with Hobbes, that the universe is merely a collection of random atoms. Instead, he holds, as do all the Deists, "that everything is governed, ordered, or regulated for the best, by a designing principle or mind, necessarily good and permanent."[6]

The optimistic appraisal of nature extends itself to human nature. Is it conceivable, he asks, that a beneficent God would create men whose nature was at war with itself or with others of his kind? The harmony found throughout the universe is also found in man. The basis of this natural harmony between men, and Shaftesbury's main line of defense against Hobbes, La Rochefoucauld, and Mandeville, is found in man's natural sociability, or, as he sometimes calls it, the herding principle.

> If eating and drinking be natural, herding is so too. If any appetite or sense be natural, the sense of fellowship is the same. If there be anything of nature in that affection which is between the sexes, the affection is certainly as natural towards the consequent offspring themselves . . . . thus a class or tribe is gradually formed; a public is recognized . . . .[7]

The recognition of the principle of natural sociability enables Shaftesbury to rescue the passions from those who see them as merely self-serving and to argue that there is a natural harmony between the individual and his society.

Shaftesbury divides the passions into three groups. The first, which he calls the "natural affections," lead to the good of the public. The second group, called the "self-affections," lead only to the good of the individual; and the last group, which he calls the "unnatural affections," lead to the injury of the individual and the public.[8] In opposition to the egoists Shaftesbury has postulated that some affections can naturally lead the individual to pursue the good of the public with no prior consideration of his own welfare or with no prior religious sentiment.

Shaftesbury must also show that there is no necessary conflict between the natural affections (public) and the self-affections (private). He argues that the public affections bring much satisfaction to the individual and that conversely the private affections are needed by the public. In both cases the emphasis is on a harmonious and balanced, rather than an antagonistic, relationship. Thus it is possible that the public affections may actually be too strong and upset the proper harmony. Shaftesbury shows this possibility by using the example of a pity "so overcoming as to destroy its own end, and prevent the succor and relief required."[9] The balance between public and private concerns can also be disturbed if the private affections are too weak, "For if a creature be self-neglectful and insensible of danger, or if he want such a degree of passion in any kind as is useful to preserve, sustain, or defend himself, this must certainly be esteemed vicious in regard of the design and end of nature."[10] The important point is that Shaftesbury denies that the natural private concerns of an individual properly understood are in opposition to the interests of the public.

Shaftesbury argues that the egoistic interpretation of man would be correct only if man lived a solitary existence. But this is not the case. Men gather together and form a larger system. A naturally sociable animal is dependent upon others not only for his material existence, but also for emotional satisfaction. This interdependence means that it is a contradiction to do good to oneself, but harm to the community. Thus, "to be well affected towards the public interest and one's own is not only consistent but inseparable; and that moral rectitude or virtue must accordingly be the advantage, and vice the injury and disadvantage of every creature."[11]

It would, however, be incorrect to think that Shaftesbury rests morality on the enlightened self-interest of men who help the community only because it benefits them. Men have a moral sense which compels them to reflect upon their actions and affections, and, in the same way that an esthetic sense immediately distinguishes beauty from ugliness and moves men toward beauty, the moral sense recognizes the proper mix of "natural affections" and the "self-affections," distinguishes vice from virtue, and moves men to prefer virtue.

Is there then . . . a natural beauty of figures? and is there not as natural a one of actions? No sooner the eye opens upon figures, the ear to sounds, then straight the beautiful results and grace and harmony are known and acknowledged. No sooner are actions viewed, no sooner the human affections and passions discovered . . . then straight an inward eye distinguishes, and sees the fair and shapely . . . the amiable and admirable, apart from the deformed . . . or the despicable. How is it possible therefore not to own that as these distinctions have their foundation in nature, the discernment itself is natural, and from nature alone.[12]

A man of good breeding, a virtuous man, does not act properly because the public interest is his own, but because his moral sense distinguishes right from wrong and compels him to act rightly. Thus virtue consists in the disinterested pursuit of the public good as approved by the moral sense. "To love the public, to study universal good, and to promote the interest of the whole world, as far as lies within our power is surely the height of goodness."[13] Disinterestedness is so important that even if a man's actions benefit the public, "if at bottom it be selfish affections alone which moves him, he is himself still vicious."[14]

Though Shaftesbury and the more religiously orthodox found in the reforming societies differ in important respects, it is clear that there are certain positions common to them both. In fact, one might say that while the ideologists of the reforming societies defend public-spiritedness by theological and, in some cases, historical arguments, Shaftesbury provides a moral psychology to buttress the arguments for public virtue. Disinterested acts aimed at the public good define virtue for both. Arguments against luxury, avarice, covetousness, and vanity are found in Shaftesbury just as they are found in the orthodox.[15] And, most important, although Shaftesbury has separated morality from religion, he has maintained its close alliance with politics. He has accepted it as obvious that "morality and good government go together."[16]

Nothing seems more certain to draw Mandeville's criticism than the kind of moral interpretation of social life found in Shaftesbury. The description of some of man's passions as naturally altruistic, the belief in the existence of an innate moral sense, and the derivation of society from virtue are all in sharp contrast to Mandeville's position. Shaftesbury's call for public-spiritedness and his criticism of luxury and avarice show Mandeville that Shaftesbury fails to understand the actual springs of action and persists in the illusion that virtue must play a role in social life. As a result, Shaftesbury is led to condemn the passions that make a prosperous mercantile community possible. In short, he is unable to see the distinction between the principles of commerce and virtue.

One of the most proper Victorians, Sir Leslie Stephen, has described Mandeville's reaction to Shaftesbury in this way.

He [Mandeville] ruthlessly destroys the fine coating of varnish which Shaftesbury has bestowed upon human nature, and shows us with a grin the hideous elements that are fermenting underneath. The grin is simply detestable; but we cannot quite deny the facts.[17]

Mandeville begins his attempt to remove the fine varnish that Shaftesbury has used on human nature in "A Search into the Nature of Society," which was appended to the *Fable*, vol. 1, in 1723.

In his opposition to the movement for the reformation of manners Mandeville had only to argue that virtue through self-denial, which both the reformers and Mandeville accepted as the definition of virtue, was impossible for most men, and that this virtue was in any case irrelevant to the growth or maintenance of society. Against Shaftesbury Mandeville was able to begin from a slightly different tack, criticizing Shaftesbury because he "imagines that men without any trouble or violence upon themselves may be naturally virtuous . . . and imagines that a man of sound understanding . . . may . . . govern himself by his reason with as much ease and readiness as a good rider manages a well taught horse by the bridle."[18] The orthodox reformers, because they held self-denial to be necessary to virtue and to be difficult to accomplish, made it easier for Mandeville to show how little moral action mattered in social life. Shaftesbury's doctrine of a natural moral sense does not begin with an awareness of the weakness of fallen man and, thus, constitutes a serious threat to Mandeville's ideas.

Mandeville's criticism of the moral sense begins by considering Shaftesbury's position that the objects of the moral sense are "standards of moral truth firmly established in nature herself."[19] Against this epistemological view Mandeville argues a rather standard pyrrhonist position, which undoubtedly owes much to Bayle. Mandeville begins by considering the difficulty we have in reaching agreement on the worth of a wide variety of objects. In painting, for example, although a common standard exists (the imitation of nature) men disagree about the value of works of art. Disagreement among florists on the beauty of different flowers shows we do no better when considering the works of nature itself. The general fickleness of mankind is betrayed in the changing fashions in clothes. Even in matters of utmost importance such as religion, the existence of pagans, Mohammedans, and Christians shows the inability of men to decide upon religious truth. The disagreement between polygamists and monogamists shows that "In morals there is no greater certainty."[20] Mandeville concludes that moral judgments like all other judgments are based on custom. Thus, "it is manifest then that the hunting after the pulchrum and honestum is not much better than a wild goose chase" (p. 331).

The doctrine of an innate moral sense, Mandeville argues, serves only to hide man's real nature from himself. "The imagining notions that men may be virtuous without self denial," in Mandeville's eyes, "are a vast inlet to hypocrisy which being once made habitual, we must not only deceive others, but likewise become altogether unknown to ourselves" (p. 331). If the mistaken ideas of Shaftesbury became universal they would ruin the wealth and power of the state. The social virtues recommended by Shaftesbury do not prepare men for "fighting for their country, or labouring to retrieve any national losses" (p. 332). The calmness and moderation found in the *Characteristics* "are good for nothing but to breed drones . . . . they would never fit him [man] for labour and assiduity, or stir him to great achievements and perilous undertakings . . ." (p. 333). Shaftesbury has simply refused to recognize those individual qualities of self-centeredness, morally called vicious, which are absolutely necessary to motivate men to undertake the labor and risks that make a rich and powerful nation.

It was not a natural moral sense or disinterested love of mankind that built society and compelled men to labor; it was one of his vices – pride. The natural desire for idleness found in man was overcome only by the stronger passion of pride. In "The Enquiry into the Origin of Moral Virtue" (1714), Mandeville has shown the importance of pride in the attempt by politicians to organize men into society. Now, in the "Search into the Nature of Society" (1723), Mandeville tries to demonstrate that the natural herding principle, which is so important in Shaftesbury, is another manifestation of pride.

Certainly it is true, says Mandeville, that men love company, but "does not man love company, as he does everything else, for his own sake . . .?" (p. 341). Men associate together for two self-interested reasons. First, they hope that their high opinion of themselves will be confirmed by their associates. Therefore, though they occasionally give pleasures to others, they do so only in order that they will be flattered in return. Second, men become aware that only through association can their material wants be satisfied. In one of his most quoted lines, he summarizes these arguments by stating: "The sociableness of man arises from these two things, viz. the multiplicity of his desires, and, the continual opposition he meets with in his endeavors to gratify them" (p. 344).

To counter Shaftesbury's claim that the origin of society resides in natural sociability and to put forward his own ideas on the origin of society, Mandeville resorts to a speculative anthropology and the fiction of a state of nature. He first considers man in that state possessed of all the natural qualities he thinks Shaftesbury attributes to man. What would be the motive, he asks, for these men, possessed of "amiable virtues and loving qualities," to undergo the hardships necessary to build society? According to Mandeville, "In such a golden age no reason or probability can be alleged why mankind ever should have raised themselves into such large societies as there have been in the world . . . . it is impossible to name a trade, art, science, dignity or employment that would not be superfluous in such a blessed state" (pp. 346–347).

Mandeville's own vision of early man outside civil society is considerably more harsh. The state of nature would be peaceful only during the first and second generations when the natural superiority of the original parents would impose order. This peace would end as soon as the original parents died and their sons began to fight among themselves. Because man can act only with a view toward satisfying himself and because man has so many appetites to satisfy, "there is not in the world a more unfit creature for society than man; a hundred of them that should all be equal, under no subjection, or fear of any superior upon earth could never live together awake two hours without quarrelling" (pp. 347–348). Peace returns only after the artifice of government reimposes the order once maintained by the original parents. And government is only one example of the way in which artifice is needed to cope with the "wants, imperfections, and the variety of his [man's] appetites" (p. 347).

Mandeville not only opposed Shaftesbury's view of man but, more generally, he challenged his hymn to nature. Throughout Mandeville we find an emphasis on the insufficiency of nature and the need for artifice to order nature so that it can provide man with his needs. Mandeville goes so far as to say that "everything is evil, which art and experience have not taught us to turn into a blessing" (p. 345).

In this short essay Mandeville has sketched his disagreement with Shaftesbury and specifically his criticism of the moral sense. He has argued that our understanding of morality demands that virtue be accompanied by a victory over nature, i.e., self-denial, which he says cannot be found in Shaftesbury. The moral sense, according to Mandeville, is also deficient because of its failure to recognize the importance of self-love in human nature and human relationships. This error is profound because a powerful and prosperous state can be built only upon the recognition of the importance of tapping the desires of egoistic men.

Driving home the true nature of men, the only secure basis on which to build society, and countering the ideas of Shaftesbury were so important that five years after the 1723 edition of the *Fable*, Mandeville published a series of six essays in dialogue form, which he called *The Fable of the Bees*, vol. 2. In the preface Mandeville makes it clear that one of the characters in the dialogue represents his own position, while the other has "found great delight in my Lord Shaftesbury's polite manner and writing."[21] In the last half of the second volume of the *Fable*, Mandeville expands his discussion of the ideas found in the "Search into the Nature of Society" and continues his attack on Shaftesbury.

He begins by criticizing attempts to read too many characteristics back into man's nature. The Hobbesian position that "man is born unfit for society" (p. 177) as well as the position of Shaftesbury that man has an innate affection for his fellows are both dismissed by Mandeville, who is unable to find in natural man either a natural aversion to or an affection for others of his species. Moreover, Mandeville argues that neither reason nor speech can be attributed to early man. The refusal to find these qualities in natural man is part of Mandeville's emphasis on artifice and development. Because Mandeville imagines man's history to be extremely long, he is able to posit that the qualities which we now associate with man were absent in his early years. Reasoning, speaking, and associating may be potential in early man, but they require long periods before experience and education are able to bring them to fruition.

Mandeville uses two analogies to convey this complex understanding of the relations between nature, artifice, and evolution. In one he compares the process by which individuals form society to the process by which grapes are turned into wine. While grapes always carry the potential of being converted to wine, the actual process is not natural or spontaneous, but requires the skill and artifice that can be learned only after many years.

> . . . the fitness of man for society, beyond other animals, is something real, but it is hardly perceptible in individuals, before great numbers of them are joyn'd together, and artfully managed . . . . Every grape contains a small quantity of juice, and when great heaps are squeez'd together, they yield a liquor, which by skillful management may be made into wine [p. 188].

Thus it is only as men learn by experience over many years how to think and speak that they learn how to live together. "Man becomes sociable," he states, "by living together in society" (p. 189). Against Shaftesbury's attempt to explain society and its achievements by recourse to man's natural sociability and innate reasonableness, Mandeville wants to explain society as the artificial creation of self-interested men.

In the third dialogue in the *Fable*, vol. 2, Mandeville considers the art of shipmaking in order to show that

> we often ascribe to the excellency of man's genius, and the depth of his penetration, what is in reality owing to length of time, and the experience of many generations . . . [p. 142].

Mandeville makes three main points about the development of man's sailing and shipbuilding capacity, which are applicable to all areas of human endeavor. The first is that the improvements in shipbuilding were made by "active, stirring, and laborious men, such as will put their hand to the plough, try experiments, and give all their attention to what they are about" (p. 144). Improvements were not made by philosophers or scientists, who usually are "fond of retirement, hate business and take delight in speculation" (p. 144).

Second, these active men of ordinary capacities were able to make improvements because they worked only on a particular problem. The notion that tasks must be "divided and subdivided" (p. 142) is, of course, the doctrine of the division of labor, and Mandeville is justly famous for his realization that the division of labor is crucial for material development.[22] But it is also interesting to note that the division of labor serves as an important point in Mandeville's argument with Shaftesbury. The division of labor helps Mandeville explain the development of mankind from its originally savage state to the skilled builder of wonders like a Man of War without recourse to an optimistic view of the nature of man. One might speculate that Mandeville developed his ideas about the division of labor only under the necessity of countering Shaftesbury.

Third, Mandeville points out that these improvements made by ordinary men working on specific tasks needed generations before they could be brought together to build a Man of War. Mandeville's awareness of the long history of mankind's development sets him off from his contemporaries and is one of his contributions to social thought.[23] And like the division of labor, it enables Mandeville to account for mankind's present material wealth while allowing him to maintain his belief in the self-interestedness of man and the importance of artifice over nature.

The emphasis on mankind's long period of development is also consistent with Mandeville's theory of knowledge. Throughout his work and especially in the *Treatise of the Hypocondriak and Hysterick Passions* (1711), Mandeville argues against the position that men have innate ideas, can understand a priori, or can penetrate to first principles.[24] Because "Physicians, with the rest of mankind, are wholly ignorant of the first principles and constitutent parts of things,"[25] they must rely on "observation, plain observation"[26] in order to understand the mechanical operations of the body. Quite self-consciously Mandeville holds the empiricist theory of knowledge made popular by John Locke. "The brain of a child," he states, "newly born, is carte blanche; . . . [so that] we have no ideas, which we are not obliged for to our senses" (p.168). Our knowledge comes only through observations received by the senses over the course of time. Men, Mandeville concludes, are able to gain knowledge only through "unwearied observation, judicious experience, and arguing from facts a posteriori . . ." (p. 164).

It is now possible to see that in Mandeville's handling of the relationships between the self-interested view of man, the empiricist theory of knowledge, the division of labor, and the awareness of mankind's long history he has developed a coherent alternative to the ideology of public-spiritedness found in the reforming societies and Shaftesbury. Mandeville is able to explain the development and maintenance of society as the result of self-interested, prideful men who in the pursuit of power, glory, and wealth devote themselves to particular tasks and by the experience gained over time learn to accomplish these tasks in improved ways and learn to live in relative harmony with one another. In the same way that an individual is able to learn by the experience of many years, society learns over time to integrate these small improvements and to progress materially. Throughout, Mandeville emphasizes custom and experience over nature, and the necessity for a strong government which can use men's fear and pride to keep the peace. Moreover, this theory of development applies equally to manners or manufacturing.

This general outline of the development of society is complemented in the second volume of the *Fable* by a more specific inquiry into mankind's history. Because Shaftesbury believes that the natural affection for others, the basis of society, first manifested itself in the family and then spread itself out to include the extended family and society, Mandeville is specific in arguing that the origins of society cannot be found in the family. Thus, he points out again, as he did in the "Search into the Nature of Society" (1723), that the binding power of the family ends with the death of the first father. Though Mandeville admits that one cannot be certain in these matters (he always understands his anthropology to be merely speculative), it is his best judgment that the first step toward society was taken in response to the threat posed by wild animals. If one considers man's love for ease and security as well as his helplessness in this early state, man's selfish desire for protection against wild animals can be seen as a sufficient motive for man to enter into social relationships.

Unfortunately, the associations necessitated by the threat of wild animals are not permanent. Since natural man is solicitous only of his own narrow self-interest, "he would do anything he has a mind to do, without regard to the consequences it would be to others" (p.164). One is reminded of the passage in Rousseau in which a primitive member of a hunting party leaves his post at the first sight of a hare that could serve as his meal.[27] In this state man cooperates with others only so long as it is in his immediate interest.

The sporadic associations of men in response to the threat of animals leads to the second step to society, for it brings man into contact with an even greater adversary – other men. "The second step to society," according to Mandeville, "is that danger men are in from one another: for which we are beholden to that staunch principle of pride and ambition, that all men are born with."[28] The groups that had banded together would begin to quarrel as soon as the threat had passed. At first, the results of these fights would be stronger bands swallowing up the weaker. Eventually, leaders would emerge who would understand that discord hindered their ambitions to lead great numbers of men. In order to remedy this discord they would promulgate laws.

The effect of the laws promulgated by ambitious leaders depends upon the clearness of the laws and the ability of large groups to know and understand them. None of these conditions could be met until laws were able to be recorded. The third step to society is then the invention of letters. Mandeville lays great emphasis on the necessity of laws because of their ability to limit or, at least, channel the egoistic desires of mankind. He states clearly that it is "inconsistent with the nature of human creatures, that any number of them should live together in tolerable concord, without laws or government" (p. 309).

The introduction of written laws has considerable importance. Property and personal safety can be secured only after laws are written and government established. But once property is secure men are provided with an added incentive to work and grow rich. Now men devote themselves to specific economic tasks in a division of labor that quickens the pace of progress. It is only after society begins to grow prosperous that the arts and sciences flourish. Perhaps we can also surmise that at this point, immediately following the introduction of writing, the moralists described by Mandeville in "An Enquiry into the Origin of Moral Virtue" (1714) begin in earnest their attempts to use pride to flatter men into more civilized standards of conduct.

Mandeville's specific attempt to provide a speculative anthropology, a history of mankind's development, illustrates some important points. He views the idea of a golden age as the result of pride, which bars men from considering their own mean origins. The history of man is not that of a fall from a golden age, but instead the history of a progressive material (not moral) development based on the uncountable small advances made by selfish men. The attempt to show how small a role virtue actually plays in the world is accompanied by the attempt to separate accurately that which is acquired and artificial from that which is natural. According to Mandeville one cannot think of speech, reason, ethics, or religion as natural to men. Just as important is Mandeville's emphasis on the importance of strong laws and government to the founding and maintenance of society.

Mandeville seems to understand that his criticism of Shaftesbury is also a criticism of a world-view common to a specific social class which he calls the *Beau Monde* and which we might generally refer to as the aristocracy. This attitude is clearly apparent as early as the *Female Tatler* with its defense of the Laborios of the world and its criticism of the notions of honor put forward by Colonel Worthy. In the first dialogue of the *Fable*, vol. 2, there is a discussion concerning styles of art and esthetic philosophies which can serve as a general introduction to Mandeville's anti-aristocratic outlook, and which places him in a current of thought in this period critical of the aristocratic modes of thought.

Mandeville has the members of the dialogue consider the differences between two paintings of the nativity scene, one by a Dutch painter and the other in the Italian style. Horatio, the young man taken with Shaftesbury's ideas, attacks the realistic portrayal of the nativity scene in the Dutch painting.

> In a country stable . . . there is nothing but filth and nastiness, or vile abject things not fit to be seen, at least not capable of entertaining persons of quality . . . . the representation of mean and abject things . . . either breeds contempt, or are insignificant . . . . the higher we can carry the excellency of our species, the more those beautiful images will fill noble minds with worthy and suitable ideas of their own dignity [pp. 34–36].

It was not necessary for Mandeville to stretch Shaftesbury's ethical ideas to apply them to art. As we have seen there is an intimate connection in Shaftesbury's own mind between a moral and an esthetic sense. Furthermore, Shaftesbury's work had a direct influence on theories of art at this time. He sided with and was used by those who argued that art had a moral purpose, which was "the representation of human action in its superior forms – heroic and sublime."[29]

These arguments are rebutted by Fulvia, clearly representing Mandeville's view, who objects to "turning the stable of a country inn into a place of extraordinary magnificence."[30] She states:

> A picture then pleases me best when the art in such a manner deceives my eye, that without making any allowances, I can imagine I see the things in reality which the painter has endeavoured to represent . . . for no body can please my eye that affronts my understanding.[31]

In the same way that Mandeville objected to moral and social theories that deluded man about his nature, he objected here to an esthetic theory that did the same.

Mandeville's preference for more realistic art is not surprising. Even as early as his first work, the translation of La Fontaine's *Fables*, the changes he made in translating tended to emphasize explicitness, earthiness, and straightforwardness.[32] Throughout Mandeville's work we find stories depicting chimney sweeps, common tradesmen, tipplers, and other low lifes. The kind of painting approved by Mandeville, and of which his earthy stories seem to be the equivalent in prose, would seem to be the genre paintings and prints of artists like Brouwer and Ostade, which characterized Dutch art in the last half of the seventeenth century and with which Mandeville must have been familiar as a young man growing up in Holland.

In England at this time the genre tradition was carried on most notably by William Hogarth. Though Hogarth did not paint low genre, his desire to "depict what he saw with his own eyes"[33] brought him into conflict with Shaftesbury's more aristocratic esthetic ideals. In fact, according to Hogarth's biographer, Ronald Paulson, Hogarth "completely reversed the Shaftesburyian paradigm" (p.120). Instead of depicting the heroic and sublime as ideals to be copied by all men, Hogarth thought, "The only way . . . to deal with the heroic in modern bourgeois-sentimental life was to depict it as a subversive force . . . . He accordingly displaces the heroic level to the false ideals that are embodied in fashionable aristocratic shapes, customs, swords, gestures . . ." (pp. 121–122). One of the most explicit demonstrations of Hogarth's treatment of the aristocracy can be seen in his paintings of John Gay's satirical play *The Beggar's Opera* (pp. 73–84).

In the same way that Hogarth was drawn to Gay's satirical treatment of the aristocracy in *The Beggar's Opera*, the last line of which was "that the lower sort of people have their vices in a degree as well as the rich, and they are punished for theirs," so too was Mandeville. In the preface to the *Fable*, vol. 2, Mandeville explicitly likened his work to Gay's. Mandeville argued that it was just as wrongheaded to blame him for vice as it was to blame Gay for highwaymen (which some did). Like Gay, Mandeville averred, he sought only to expose the vices of man. Mandeville's interest in the theater is continued in the text of the *Fable*, vol. 2, where immediately after the discussion of styles of painting his spokesmen defend the theater for its realism and criticize, as did Gay in *The Beggar's Opera*, the Italian opera.

Within certain limits, it is possible to see heroic-history painting, Italian opera, and the moral theory of Shaftesbury as part of a characteristically aristocratic world-view which to various degrees is being satirized and criticized in the works of Hogarth, Gay, and Mandeville. However, there is an important difference between these works of Gay and Hogarth, however realistic, and Mandeville's. The works of Gay and Hogarth remain mostly satirical, critical of the aristocracy mainly for its hypocrisy. Because neither Gay nor Hogarth repudiates the idea that art should serve a moral purpose, their work, unlike Mandeville's, is consistent with the ideals of public-spiritedness.

Mandeville's entire attack on Shaftesbury's moral pyschology can, as I have indicated, also be seen as a critique of the aristocratic world. Among the men of the *Beau Monde*, according to Mandeville,

> virtue . . . is a very fashionable word, and some of the most luxurious are extremely fond of the amiable sound; tho' they mean nothing by it, but a great veneration for whatever is courtly or sublime, and an equal aversion to everything, that is vulgar or unbecoming . . . whilst the votaries of it deny themselves no pleasure, they can enjoy, either fashionably or in secret.[34]

In this respect he is following in the tradition of the Jansenists and La Rochefoucauld who tried to debunk the heroic aristocratic vision of Corneille, for example, and the Frondeurs in the preceeding century. Like the Jansenists Mandeville begins with a strict definition of virtue and follows with an acute psychological analysis, which uncovers the omnipotence of self-love. But his analysis goes beyond satire by calling into question the standards on which satire is based. For Mandeville the point is not just that honor and concern for the public are ideals by which many men fail to live. Mandeville opposes to the sublime and virtuous ideals of the *Beau Monde* a coherent set of values based on the demands of a commercial nation.

A specifically critical account of the aristocratic view of life can be found in that part of the *Fable*, vol. 2, where Horatio and Cleomenes agree to inquire into the motives of a hypothetical aristocrat endowed with all the virtuous characteristics suitable to a man of high position. Horatio believes that "no men upon earth . . . are more courteous, humane or polite than persons of high birth, that enjoy large possessions, and known seats of their ancestors, men illustrious by descent, that have been used to grandeur and titles of honor from their infancy . . ." (p. 66). Cleomenes, Mandeville's spokesman, on the other hand, wants to show that "a most beautiful superstructure may be raised upon a rotten and despicable foundation" (p. 64).

The discussion of aristocratic virtue is guided by Cleomenes to the consideration of the rules of honor and dueling, topics which Mandeville has written about since the *Female Tatler* (1709–10). What is it, inquires Mandeville's spokesman, that compels a well-tempered man to engage in such violence, and what provides him with the courage to undergo a duel? The answer provided by Horatio that it is his "natural courage . . . and the rectitude of his manners" (p. 82) is not satisfactory. Cleomenes points out that the demands of honor are contrary to the written laws of the country and the laws of God.[35] The Christian religion clearly defines the taking of another man's life as a sin. Yet so completely do the rules of honor bind that even clergymen contemptuously label a man who refuses to stand and fight a coward. The motivations of the aristocratic man, therefore, cannot be found in high ethical considerations, but must, as with all other men, be found in pride. The "social virtues that Lord Shaftesbury has hinted at . . . [come] from no better principle than vain-glory."[36]

Not only is honor not based on religious virtue, Mandeville also wants to show that it is in no sense natural. Cleomenes asks Horatio, the defender of Shaftesbury and the aristocracy, to consider the courage he showed in a duel and the fear he felt on a ship in a storm. Education and custom, Mandeville wants to say, are capable of fixing honor and shame on different objects. Men in one culture may feel shame for committing acts that would bring honor to a man in a different culture.

Shaftesbury has once again taken characteristics to be natural which Mandeville shows to be the artificial results of custom.

In the process of debunking aristocratic virtue Mandeville adds one of the most important refinements to his analysis of human nature. He distinguishes, first in the *Fable*, vol. 2, between that instinct in all animals that compels them to preserve themselves and their young – which he calls self-love – and the instinct in all animals to overvalue themselves, which he calls self-liking.[37] The doctrine that society comes from the vices of man demands that Mandeville establish a principle other than that of self-preservation, hardly a vice, on which to base pride, avarice, envy, etc. Self-preservation, or as Mandeville calls it, self-love, only compels man to "scrape together everything it wanted for sustenance, provide against the injuries of the air, and do everything to make itself and young ones secure."[38] But nature has not stopped with a general instinct of self-preservation. It has added an instinct "by which every individual values itself above its own worth" (p.130). This innate desire, called self-liking, makes man seek "for opportunities, by gestures, looks and sounds, to display the value it has for itself, superior to what it has for others" (p.133).

The instinct of self-liking has an important function. It assists in the preservation of the species by furnishing man with "that relish we have for life, even when it is not worth having . . . . it doubles our happiness in prosperity and buoys us up against the frowns of adverse fortune" (p.135). Self-liking is able to turn aside the strongest inclinations of nature. Thus, for example, Mandeville attributes the existence of politeness, so important to the aristocracy, to the existence of self-liking because it gives man an interest in listening to the opinions of others in the hopes these will confirm his own high opinion of himself.

Mandeville's interest in unmasking aristocratic virtue continued to the end of his life, and in his last full-length work, *An Enquiry into the Origin of Honour* (1732), he explored further the origins of honor and its relationship to self-liking. Mandeville opens this work with a restatement of the distinction between self-liking and self-love and by emphasizing that both vicious and virtuous actions have their origin in self-liking. As one of the interlocutors says to Mandeville's spokesman:

> We are all born with a passion manifestly distinct from self love; that, when it is moderate and well regulated, excites in us the love of praise . . . and when it is excessive . . . gives offense to others . . . and is called pride. As there is no word or expression that comprehends all the different effects of this same cause, this passion you have made one, viz. self liking, by which you mean the passion in general.[39]

Mandeville proceeds to argue that honor, so far from being the natural virtue of the well-born, has its psychological origins in self-liking, "that great value, which all individuals set upon their own person" (p. 3). Thus, to honor someone is to gratify his sense of self-liking. "Honour." Mandeville says, "is a compliment we make to those who act, have, or are what we approve of, it is a term of art to express our concurrence with others, and agreement with them in their sentiment concerning the esteem and value they have for themselves" (pp. 8–9). Conversely, to show dishonor is to show that we disagree with the high value we know someone places on himself. Moreover, because we give honor only to those men or qualities of which we also approve, honor is rooted not only in the self-liking of the person honored, but also in the self-liking of the person who pays honor.

Once Mandeville has unmasked the psychological origins of honor, he attempts to unmask its social origins by tracing it to the machinations of moralists who desired to control men. It appears that moralists in order to subdue men first tried to teach virtue and flatter men into denying their passions. Clearly, this method would affect only a very few. Along with this ploy moralists sought to use the fear men naturally had of invisible causes, which gave rise to religion, to curb men's passions. The chief use of religion, according to Mandeville, is to appeal to or invoke an invisible power in promises of allegiance or loyalty. But Mandeville is explicit in denying the opinion so widely held that religion could adequately provide a cement for society. Because men are so concerned with immediate pleasures and pains, future considerations have little effect on their actions. It is because death rarely enters the minds of men that religion has so little impact. In fact, the only reason politicians use religion is because no one would obey a government if it contradicted what all men know to be true – that there is a God.

Just as all skills are improved only over time, moralists learned to use honor and shame only after virtue and religion had proved unsatisfactory methods for subduing men. The "little power which Christianity has over our hearts" and "our incapacity of subduing strong passion" demanded that moralists find another solution (p. 80). Thus honor "seems to have been an invention to influence men, whom religion had no power over" (p.15). The great benefit derived from using honor and shame to tame men is that self-denial is not required. The desire to be honored and the fear of shame are rooted in the notions men have about their own worth. The possibility of regulating men does not therefore depend upon the ability to contradict the passion of self-liking, but instead requires that self-liking actually be increased, a task consistent with the nature of men. Men are taught to worship themselves. Moralists through education are able to establish the kinds of behavior that will enhance and lower the self-image of a man. Moreover, it is not possible to escape the demands of honor, simply because it is not possible to escape one's self-image. Even when men are alone or are able to act without fear of physical punishment their concern with their self-image will serve to regulate their actions.

Mandeville gives two examples of the ways in which honor and shame have been used to control the actions of men. Moralists have made honor in a woman dependent upon chaste behavior, while in men honor has been attached to courageous action in warfare. An unfortunate effect of this education has been the identification of honor and courage with dueling. It would be a mistake, according to Mandeville, to attempt to curb dueling by seeking to restrain or conquer pride and anger. Not only would such an attempt at requiring self-denial fail, but to the extent it might succeed it would destroy the passions necessary to military power. The only way to abolish dueling would be for moralists to educate men so that dueling was made to appear inconsistent with self-esteem, that is, honor.

Throughout Mandeville's work there is considerable confusion and ambiguity over his use of the terms "moralist" and "politician" as well as confusion over what he means by "pride." In both cases there seem to be situations where moralists and pride are destructive of social order and others where they have seemed absolutely necessary to the evolution and maintenance of society. In the *Enquiry into the Origin of Honour* (1732), Mandeville begins to clarify what he has meant when he talked of moralists and politicians. According to Mandeville, these are

> All that, having studied human nature, have endeavored to civilize man, and render them more and more tractable, either for ease of governors . . . or else the temporal happiness of society in general . . . . Human wisdom is the child of time. It was not the contrivance of one man, nor could it have been the business of a few years . . . [p. 91].

This statement does not invalidate Mandeville's emphasis upon the artificial creation of society and the need for an imposed order; rather, it simply emphasizes that time and experience are important in the work of moralists and politicians, as they are in all other human undertakings. Moreover, because this statement of Mandeville's makes clear that society is not the creation of one set of moralists or politicians who intervened at a particular point in history, it emphasizes the *constant* need for moralists and politicians who draw upon the work of their predecessors to work for the maintenance of society. These men are indispensable because each new generation of men require to be tamed anew.

However, to see that "moralists and politicians" are not used by Mandeville as a *deus ex machina*, in the style of Rousseau's Legislator, does not clear up the ambiguity in his use of these terms. Certainly the moralists found in the reforming societies and those like Shaftesbury who have deluded man about his nature have not worked for the betterment of society. The confusion over the proper role of the moralists is tied to the confusion over the proper understanding of pride, for the value of the moralists is dependent upon the value of their teaching. In order to distinguish between the two kinds or uses of pride and moralists we need go no further than Mandeville's central position – the incompatibility of commerce and virtue.

In Bickerstaff and Shaftesbury can be found an optimistic view of man, heavily influenced by Stoic ideas and particularly compatible with the outlook of an aristocratic view of the world, which denies the essentially egoistic and prideful nature of man. To Mandeville this view is the result of a pride that does not understand itself and that deludes men into thinking they can act virtuously, deny their passions if necessary, elevate themselves above the hustle and bustle of commercial life, and in so doing find peace and contentment. From *The Grumbling Hive* (1705) on throughout his work, Mandeville has argued that these views are destructive of mercantile society, that "Content . . . is the bane of industry."[40]

The alternative understanding of pride and egoism as part of man's instinctual make up is more akin to French *moralistes'* ideas and more compatible with a commercial style of life.[41] Within this lifestyle there is a frank acceptance of man's egoistic nature, the desire of all men to outshine their neighbors and glorify themselves by the accumulation of wealth and the fine clothes and houses that wealth can buy. This pride can provide the motivation for men to labor and to fight to establish a rich and powerful mercantile state.

These two different attitudes toward pride are characteristic of two different groups of moralists. Those in the reforming societies and the authors of the *Tatler* did not accept the inevitability of egoism, the instinctual nature of self-liking, and taught that society depended upon the denial of pride and the other passions. In Shaftesbury, according to Mandeville, man was deluded even further by the idea that society was the natural outgrowth of a natural altruism; thus he did not even recognize the pride that the reformers had at least argued had to be overcome.

Consider, on the other hand, the moralists portrayed by Mandeville in his speculative anthropology. In "An Enquiry into the Origin of Moral Virtue" (1714) these moralists, like Mandeville himself understand that the passions cannot be conquered. They do not hold out "vain eutopia[s] seated in the brain"[42] which foresee societies free from vanity and selfishness. Instead of attempting to convince men to renounce their pride, they use the pride and self-interest of men and thereby begin to civilize mankind.

# Chapter 4 Mandeville and Mercantilism

The moral interpretation of social life, the belief that public and private morality are responsible for the cohesion and proper operation of society, is rejected by Mandeville. In the manner of the French *moraliste* he has unmasked seemingly virtuous activity at all levels of society, finding special satisfaction in unmasking the pretensions of the honorable. Behind each mask he has found self-interest and, if not vice alone, at least the constant mixture of virtue and vice. In the *moraliste* this brilliant cynicism and astute psychological insight were mainly focused upon the activities of the court and the high-born, and it remained a predominantly individual, moral critique, social only by implication. In Mandeville the psychological analysis of self-love is explicitly joined to a social and economic theory which, I will argue, is similar to what has been called the mercantilist conception of society.[1]

According to Eli Heckscher, "The underlying idea of mercantilism may be expressed as follows: people should be taken as they are and should be guided by wise measures in that direction which will enhance the well being of the state."[2] Mandeville has explicitly attacked the moral reformers Steele and Shaftesbury for misunderstanding the true nature of man, refusing to see him as he really is, and thereby deducing principles of social action that are incompatible with state power and state wealth – the prime objective of the mercantilist. Mandeville alone in this period openly argues that traditional moral and social thought is inconsistent with the goals of the mercantilist state. And by arguing that the vision of a moral community is impossible, he, more than any of his contemporaries, sanctions the economic measures that will enhance the glory and wealth, if not the virtue, of England.

We would not expect to find the acceptance of the economic world in a time or place that had not been awakened to the promise of material prosperity. It is then not surprising that Mandeville's acceptance of this world occurs in a period of great economic expansion. Mandeville spent his life in the two most economically advanced countries of the period –

Holland and England – during a time of enormous economic growth and invention. It is appropriate that Mandeville concerned himself with economics as well as morals, for it seems that in the early eighteenth century all of England was preoccupied with matters financial. Many have pointed out that after the peace brought by the Restoration in 1660, England turned her attention to economic reconstruction.[3] Heckscher calls the years 1660–1720 "the most eventful time in the history of English enterprises" and notes that it was characterized by an "unprecedented acceleration in the tempo of economic life."[4] More recently Ralph Davis has called the entire period from the Restoration to the American War of Independence a Commercial Revolution.[5] The last decades of the seventeenth century saw the flowering of a group of economists – Dudley North, Sir William Petty, Charles Davenant, Josiah Child, Nicholas Barbon – who for the first time began to look at economic affairs in a systematic manner.[6] In the 1690s England started for the first time to try to collect official trade statistics, and no wonder, for the scale and complexity of economic life increased in such a way as to touch the lives of all Englishmen.

Professor Davis remarks that "the attention that writers of the latter period of the seventeenth and eighteenth century gave to problems connected with overseas trade is no accident, but a testimony to its importance in English economic life."[7] One can begin to understand the importance and magnitude of the commercial revolution in the last decades of the seventeenth century by comparing the importance of English woolen exports, which traditionally accounted for the vast majority of English exports, in 1640 and 1700. Just before the English revolution woolen accounted for 80 percent of English exports, but by 1700 woolen cloth had fallen to less than half, 47 percent, of total exports.[8] In the period 1640 to 1700 total English exports increased from £2½ or 3 million to £6½ million.[9]

The great change in English trade in this period was due to the enormous increase in England's reexport trade; that is, the exportation from English ports, mainly London, to the Continent of goods first imported from the colonies. In this trade English merchants were able to act as middlemen. The reexport trade was dominated by three goods – tobacco and sugar from the Americas and calicos from India. Tobacco exports to England from Maryland and Virginia, which were 20,000 pounds in 1615, rose to 7 million in 1662–63, 9 million in 1668–69, 12 million in the late 1680s, and 22 million in 1699–1701.[10] While all of England consumed approximately 50,000 pounds in 1615, by 1699–1701 England consumed 13 million pounds and reexported to the Continent another 25 million pounds (p. 258). The trade of calicos also increased rapidly in the last decade of the century. From virtually zero before the Restoration, calico imports rose to 861,000 pounds in 1699–1701, two-thirds of which were later reexported (p. 260). In general, the reexport of sugar, tobacco, and calico at least trebled in the period 1660–1700 (pp. 265–266). According to Davis, "this was a revolution in trade" (p. 268).

The expansion in English trade in this period was dependent upon British control over her colonies and the navigation acts of 1651 and 1660, which were passed to deprive the Dutch of the new trade. These laws resulted not only in British ships carrying the trade, but also ensured that the goods from the colonies were brought to London before they were sent to the Continent. London now began to surpass the Dutch ports as the busiest in Europe. The colonies also provided a protected market for English manufacturers which, even if small and accounting for only 8 per cent of English exports, was growing rapidly (p. 261). It is not surprising, given the nature of this revolution in trade and its dependence upon government regulation, that "the later seventeenth century conception of economic freedom was neither comprehensive nor effective."[11]

The effects of this commercial revolution were felt throughout the society. The new products, made inexpensive by their volume, created new demands and habits of consumption among the English middle class.[12] The new size and pattern of trade also demanded a much larger English fleet. But even more important, this long-distance international trade attracted large amounts of capital and attracted it much faster than manufacturing did. The importance of international trade to the English economy helps account for the increase in the political power of the merchant community. It also helps explain the concentration in economic thought on the balance of payments and the identification of national interest with high exports.[13]

The quickened pace of economic activity and the need to finance wars brought on by international trade rivalries called forth new financial institutions. The invention of new and the growth of old financial institutions were so dramatic in the last decade of the seventeenth century and the first half of the eighteenth century that some have called this period a Financial Revolution.[14] For example, between 1689 and 1695 the number of joint stock companies in England rose from eleven to approximately one hundred.[15] The amount of capital invested in joint stock companies increased enormously in the first years of the eighteenth century, going from £4 million in 1695 to £20 million in 1717 to £50 million in 1720.[16] It was also in this period that fire insurance (1710) and marine insurance (1720) were developed.[17]

Perhaps even more important than the growth of the private joint stock trading companies was the development of public credit in the first half of the eighteenth century and, associated with this innovation, the founding in 1694 and subsequent growth of the Bank of England. The seemingly constant warfare in this period put a considerable strain upon the government. The impact of the war with France after the 1688 revolution was to increase the government budget two to three times.[18] Because of the inability of the system of taxation to provide the necessary funds, the government was forced to find ways to borrow money. The government debt was the subject of considerable controversy during these years, and the stock jobber who traded government securities as well as the stock of the private trading companies was its most hated figure.

The effect of these economic changes in the first half of the eighteenth century seems to have been one of general material prosperity.[19] Both manufacturing and trade showed steady growth. Agricultural output increased more dramatically so that England became the major agricultural surplus area in northwestern Europe. Because population growth was relatively slow, expansion of industry pushed up the demand for and wages of labor. The slow population growth coupled with increases in agricultural production also meant that the price of foodstuffs declined. The steady decline in interest rates for over a century until the start of the Seven Year's War shows an abundance of investable capital and is indicative of the material progress. This prosperity meant a wider selection of consumer goods and more generally "the rise of internal demand which permanently affected the level of expectation of most classes in English society."[20]

To this general prosperity there was one important exception – the small squires and gentry. According to H. J. Habakkuk the greatest change in English landownership between 1680 and 1740 was the increase in the land owned by the great families and the diminution in area owned by the small squires and gentry.[21] The need of the government to finance the wars with France played an important role in this transfer of land. The taxes levied by the government to help finance the war fell most heavily on land and on those who drew their entire income from rents. The aristocracy was not only better able to bear these taxes because larger land holdings were organized and run more efficiently, but, just as important, they were able to derive other income from their positions in government. The other way for the government to raise money for the wars – public credit – also worked to aid the great families and hurt the gentry. Whereas in earlier periods much bourgeois money was drawn into land because it was profitable, in this period much investment went into government securities, which often had a safe yield of 6 percent.[22] Isaac Kramnick has suggested that the pessimism of this age, the hatred of the new economic order, comes primarily from those parts of the literary community associated with the gentry.[23]

This pessimistic appraisal, which we have encountered in the moral reformers, focused particularly on luxury as a manifestation of corruption. It is possible to see in the attention given to luxury in the early eighteenth century in England the conflict between world-views dominated by considerations of virtue and those dominated by considerations of commerce. The moral interpretation of social life, which was characterized above all by the perception and fear of widespread corruption, saw in luxury only the desire for individual selfish gain. Men caught up in the pursuit of riches were unable to consider the good of the public. Men whose interests were only to sell to the highest bidder could sell a government office, perhaps even allegiance itself, as easily as they could sell lesser goods. The belief that widespread luxury destroyed the virtue that was necessary to the public as well as the individual's well-being was as common to Tories like Bolingbroke as it was to Real Whigs like Gordon and Trenchard. In *The Idea of a Patriot King* Bolingbroke hoped "to reinforce the spirit of liberty, to reform the morals" of men who were "debased from the love of liberty, from zeal for the honor and prosperity of their country, and from a desire of honest fame to an absolute unconcernedness for all these, to an abject submission, and to a rapacious eagerness after wealth, that may sate their avarice, and exceed the profusion of their luxury . . . ."[24] Though Bolingbroke professed a desire for prosperity, it was clearly the prosperity of an earlier era which was without merchants, stockjobbers, and public debts.

Though Bolingbroke and the radical Whigs disagreed on some political issues, they shared a belief in the importance of public-spiritedness, the perception of widespread corruption, and a rejection of luxury specifically and the new commercial world in general. Like so many others they saw in the historical example of Rome confirmation of their ideas. The rise of republican Rome according to Trenchard and Gordon was explained by its superior virtue – "it conquered by its virtues more than its arms"[25] – while the fall of Rome was laid to corruption. Thus ". . . private regards extinguished that love of liberty, that zeal and warmth, which their ancestors had shown for the interest of the public; luxury and pride became fashionable . . . and having before sold everything else, at last they sold their country."[26] In their own time, according to Trenchard and Gordon, there were men who were given over wholly to private concerns, and though they talked of public spirit, they "intend only some poor and selfish gratification of their own."[27] As examples of such selfish men Trenchard and Gordon named ". . . the trader and artificer" who encouraged "only that sort of art or ware in which he himself deals."[28] Like Bolingbroke, these Real Whigs worried that the new world of merchants and manufacturers could destroy the virtue on which a well-ordered society must depend.

The fear of luxury was not new to eighteenth-century England. For centuries it had been a platitude that luxury was immoral and harmful to the health of the individual and society. Plato tried to insulate the guardians in the *Republic* from its effects, and in the *Laws* he located his hypothetical city inland so that it would not be corrupted by excessive trade or luxury. In the Middle Ages it was thought that the presence of luxury indicated an excessive concern for material possessions and turned one's attention from more proper otherworldly concerns. The pursuit of luxury also tended to encourage men to leave their assigned station and thereby violate the great chain of being. The attack on luxury was continued in the Renaissance by Machiavelli, and he bequeathed to the republicans of seventeenth-century England a republicanism based on simplicity and equality. The arguments against luxury also used the example of the success of Sparta and of Holland in the seventeenth century to show that strength could flow from frugality. In this period of intense international rivalry the supposed effect of luxury to weaken and enfeeble a people was thought especially important.

The attack on the traditional view of luxury, which culminated in the work of Mandeville, began in earnest in the late seventeenth century on two fronts – one primarily moral in tone, the other based on economic arguments. In the Epicurean Saint-Evremond, who lived in England from 1665 to his death in 1703, we find arguments that the severity and rigor of Christian morality deform the natural instincts in man. These arguments resulted in a revaluation of luxury. Saint-Evremond opposed the rigorist morality that was suspicious of all pleasures and argued that "it is an error to condemn pleasure as *pleasure* [his emphasis], and not as they are, unjust or unlawful."[29] Far from finding injustice in luxury, he found beauty.

> Let us not play the philosopher so far, as to condemn by our austerity, the magnificence of the court . . . . we may well neglect those extravagent maxims, whose severity reforms fewer men, than it scares.
>
> If we cannot afford to be splendid, let us not accuse others of luxury. A man cannot condemn so much art and fine workmanship he sees in the world, all of which is the effect of human industry, without being fanatically severe.
>
> A man may very innocently admire the pomp of a glorious city, he may partake of the pleasures of perfume, and the satisfaction of music. In short, he may behold with delight, the delicacy of painting, and yet not violate the laws of temperance.[30]

Saint-Evremond, as we might expect, was unimpressed with the movement to reform manners. "Nothing," he said, "is more unprofitable than the wisdom of those persons who set up for reformers of the age. Tis a part a man cannot act long, without offending his friends, and rendering himself ridiculous."[31] Furthermore, he thought little of frugality. Instead, he held that "honors, reputation, riches and amours, and well managed pleasures are a mighty relief against the rigors of nature, and the miseries of life. And, indeed, the principal end for which wisdom was given us, was to direct us in the enjoyment of pleasure."[32] Following Epicurus, he counseled only that "we ought to be moderate in our pleasures."[33]

In Pierre Bayle, Mandeville's mentor, we find a combination of the moral and economic justification for luxury. Bayle, like Saint-Evremond, rejected the severity and intolerance of Christianity, and in order to debunk its rigorous ethics, he demonstrated the hypocrisy of Christians by showing how little their religious principles actually motivated their behavior. The desire for luxury among Christians was simply one more example of their hypocrisy. However, in order to show the incompatibility of Christian ethics with the natural world, Bayle used the economic argument that luxury employed many men in the state – "a moderate luxury has great benefits in a Republic; it makes money circulate, it enables the common people (*le petit peuple*) to live . . . ."[34]

The wholly economic view of luxury surfaced repeatedly in seventeenth-century France and was, according to Heckscher, an integral part of mercantilist doctrine. "Mercantilism rejected in principle any ethical attitude toward luxury. The only consideration . . . was how far a particular measure furthered or obstructed economic life."[35] Spending for luxury items that stimulated domestic production was justified as early as 1598 in the writing of Laffemas.[36] The apology for luxury on the grounds that it employed many who might otherwise be idle can also be seen in the work of Jean Pottier de Hestroye, who, writing in Bayle's and Mandeville's period, wrote that though "fashions cause unnecessary spending . . . if the rich and those who enter into luxury reduce their wealth in this way, it is certain they also support at the same time an infinity of poor families . . . ."[37] However, mercantilist principles that in some cases justified luxury spending, in other cases found good economic reasons for objecting to the purchase of luxury goods which were imported.

A more systematic defense of luxury was launched late in the seventeenth century by a group of predominantly Tory economic writers.[38] Dudley North and Nicholas Barbon, who were preeminent in this group, argued that even luxury goods purchased from abroad should not, under proper conditions, be prohibited. Since the prohibition of 1678 on French imported goods there had been a continual fight between the king and the parliament over trade with France.[39] The court and the party formed around it were generally sympathetic to the importation of French goods, if only because the customs duties which the court received from increased French trade were independent of parliamentary control. However, because so many of the French goods were luxury items, it was necessary in order to increase trade with France to justify the purchase of luxury goods that had to be imported. In 1688 when the prohibition on French goods was again put in force, after a period under James II in which the prohibition had been replaced by a tariff, Tory writers such as North and Barbon sought to defend luxury spending.

Because it was clear that individuals and families could be ruined by the immoderate purchase of luxury goods, it was necessary, in order to argue for the relaxation of the prohibition against the importation of luxury goods, to deny the analogy that likened the economics of the household to the economics of the state. Thus, in 1690 when Nicholas Barbon argued against Thomas Mun's recommendations for frugality and sumptuary laws, he rejected the supposed desirable effects of frugality by stating that ". . . this is true, of a person, but not of a nation,"[40] and "Prodigality is a vice that is prejudicial to the man, but not to trade" (p. 32). Barbon argued that a nation was enriched not only by trade for simple bodily needs, but also for those desires created by the imagination – luxuries. Moreover, Barbon saw that trade for the desires of the imagination was more advantageous and a better promoter of trade because these desires were unlimited.

> The wants of the mind are infinite, man naturally aspires, and as his mind is elevated, his senses grow more refined, and more capable of delight; his desires are enlarged, as his wants increase with his wishes, which is for everything that is rare, can gratify his senses, adorn his body and promote the ease, pleasure, and pomp of life [p. 14; see also p. 21].

Through trade sparked by changing fashions and the prodigality of the rich, everyone benefited (p. 31).

It is clear that Barbon did not have just domestic trade in mind, for he specifically tackled the problem of trade with the French. He pointed out that when England prohibited the importation of French goods, France had to respond and cease to trade with England (pp. 35–40). This reciprocal relationship meant that Englishmen who might have lived by producing goods exported to France were unemployed. Nor could it be argued, he said, that money not spent on French goods would necessarily be spent on English goods. Because most trade was for goods desired by the mind, money that would have been spent on French lace would not necessarily be spent on English lace. However, one must be careful not to read into Barbon a general theory of free trade. When a domestic industry was clearly hurt by trade, Barbon was ready to establish high custom barriers (pp. 35–40).

A year later, in 1691, Dudley North continued these arguments in his *Discourse upon Trade*. He began his chapter on money by stating that "the main spur to trade, or rather to industry and ingenuity, is the exorbitant appetites of men."[41] These appetites were not only for basic goods needed to sustain our lives, but also for the goods desired by imagination and vanity.

A tradesman sees his neighbour keep a coach, presently all his endeavors is at work to do the like, and many times is beggared by it; however the extraordinary application he made, to support his vanity, was beneficial to the public [pp. 27–28].

Emulation and vanity were not the only passions which caused men to desire luxurious goods and in the process benefit the public.

The glutton works hard to purchase delicacies, wherewith to gorge himself; the gamester, for money to venture at play; the miser, to hoard, and so others. Now in the pursuit of these appetites other men less exorbitant are benefitted [p. 27].

These desires or appetites cannot be controlled without hurting the prospects of the country for economic prosperity. North remarked that "Countries which have sumptuary laws, are generally poor" (p. 27). Like Barbon he recognized the distinction between means to enrich the family, which may include frugality, and the means to enrich the nation (p. 27). It is interesting that propositions which were put forward by Mandeville in the next three decades and which received so much criticism are found here in two tracts by Barbon and North, and received very little attention.

In Mandeville's discussion of luxury we can see both the French moral and the English economic tradition brought together. André Morize makes this point when he says of Mandeville:

He is important, because, in this fertile period, he represents the decisive moment when the French Epicurean and skeptical tradition meets the English economic tradition – and when, to the moral doctrines of Montaigne, La Rochefoucauld, Saint Evremond and Bayle are joined the more scientific theories of William Petty, Dudley North, Davenant and the others.[42]

While these two traditions have already raised most of the points Mandeville will use, and some, like the elasticity of demand found in Barbon, that he will not, Mandeville's formulation is so provocative, even scandalous, that it demanded the attention of his contemporaries. Heckscher refers to it as "the most provocative and most widely discussed formulation of this mercantilist argument that it ever received,"[43] and E. A. J. Johnson maintains that "the most significant and penetrating analysis of the disadvantages and benefits of luxury [in Hume] was precipitated by Mandeville's *Fable of the Bees*."[44]

Mandeville's first mention of luxury comes in *The Grumbling Hive: Or Knaves Turned Honest* (1705) when, in his description of the prosperous hive before virtue disastrously descended on the bees, he said: ". . . Whilst luxury / Employed a million of the poor, / And odious pride a million more."[45] Here Mandeville is making the familiar argument that luxury spending by the rich employs the poor. At the same time he is using luxury as one more example of a vice (pride, envy, and avarice are others), at least as defined by Christian rigorists, which contributes to the public good. When Mandeville wrote the first volume of *Fable of the Bees* (by adding comments to explain different parts of the original poem) he showed his continued interest in luxury. The remarks devoted to luxury and related topics such as frugality and pleasure are some of the longest in the book. In these sections he deepens the discussion, becomes more specific in his criticism, and incorporates into the discussion more economic justifications of luxury.

Mandeville begins his justification of luxury by using a familiar ploy. Just as he had defined Christian morality as rigorously as possible, he now defines necessity, the opposite of luxury, as narrowly as possible. The effect of this method is clear. It so enlarges the area of luxury that luxury encompasses almost every improvement made by man, and thereby the term is rendered useless.

> If everything is to be luxury (as in strictness it ought) that is not immediately necessary to make man subsist as he is a living creature, there is nothing else to be found in the world, no not even among the naked savages; of which it is not probable that there are any but what by this time have made some improvements upon their former manners of living . . . . this definition everybody will say is too rigorous; I am of the same opinion; but if we were to abate one inch of this severity, I am afraid we shan't know where to stop . . . . if once we depart from calling everything luxury that is not absolutely necessary to keep a man alive, then there is no luxury at all [pp. 107–108].

Mandeville buttresses this enlarged definition of luxury by examining the condition of primitive man and emphasizing the distance that separates even the lowliest Englishmen from early man. In the earliest years of mankind, man must have "fed on the fruits of the earth, without any previous preparation, and reposed himself naked like other animals on the lap of the common parent . . ." (p. 169). Should not every convenience which has since that early time made life more comfortable deserve the name "luxury"? Consider that even the coarsest, most common shirt worn by an Englishman has been the result of innumerable improvements.

> . . . What a number of people, how many different trades, and what a variety of skill and tools, must be employed to have the most ordinary Yorkshire cloth? What depth of thought and ingenuity, what tools and labour, and what length of time must it have cost, before man could learn from a seed to raise and prepare so useful a product of linen [p. 169].

That an early man would describe such a shirt as luxurious shows that the necessities of one age are the luxuries of another. And if by necessity we mean the minimum necessary to keep a man alive, the condition of primitive man, then almost all that now exists is luxury.

Having complicated the traditional view of luxury by showing how impossible it is to use the term with precision, Mandeville now proceeds to explain in more detail the economic benefits which result from luxury spending. He again points out the number of men who are employed by the luxury spending of the rich and argues that the effects of universal frugality, urged by moral reformers and some economists, would be disastrous. If men owned only one suit of clothes or refused to build new sumptuous houses as long as old ones were still standing, "masons, carpenters, bricklayers and co. would want employment, and the building trade having once destroyed, what would become of limning, carving and other arts that are ministering to luxury?" (p. 223).

But the pursuit of luxury goods that is caused by pride, vanity, and emulation affects the economy in a more general and more important way. It provides the individual with the motivation to work. The desire to equal or outshine one's neighbor by owning luxury items is one of the most important means by which a man is roused from "his natural innocence and stupidity" (p. 206). Mandeville is acutely aware of the power of envy and emulation, particularly in large cities, to compel a man to live outside of himself. Not only is there more to excite the passions, to see and to envy, in large cities, there is also more opportunity for a man to pretend to strangers that he is something he is not.

> . . . handsome apparel is a main point, fine feathers make fine birds, and people, where they are not known, are generally honored according to their clothes . . . . It is this which encourages everybody, who is conscious of his little merit, to wear clothes above his rank, especially in large and populous cities, where obscure men may hourly meet with fifty strangers to one acquaintance, and consequently have the pleasure of being esteemed by a vast majority, not as what they are, but what they appear to be [pp. 127–128].

While some moralists may be appalled at this idea, Mandeville sees its benefits, for "it is this . . . that sets the poor to work, adds spurs to industry, and encourages the skillful artificer to search after further improvements" (p. 130).

The argument that luxury weakened the strength and courage of the nation's men exercised considerable influence in Mandeville's time, and he is forced to devote many pages to the argument against it. The popularity of this view is not surprising considering its long tradition and the international rivalry of the period, which put a premium on military as well as economic skill. Mandeville begins by suggesting that the accounts of the luxury in ancient Egypt and Persia (and by implication Rome) owed more to imagination than to fact. If one were to believe such accounts "one third of the people [were] sick a-bed with surfeits; another laid up with the gout, or crippled by a more ignominious distemper; and the rest, that could go without leading, walk along the streets in petticoats" (p. 118). In the place of these wild imaginings Mandeville proposes a more realistic view based on the constancy of human nature, which teaches that "as long as men have the same appetites, the same vices will remain" (p. 118). While every society will have some who indulge to an unhealthy extent, there is little reason to believe that there will be more at one time than another. Moreover, we find the inordinate indulgence of certain passions, liquor and lust for example, in all classes, not just the rich who purchase luxury goods. There is no reason to believe that fine wines are more enervating than cheap malts, and, according to Mandeville, ". . . clean linen weakens a man no more than flannel; tapestry, fine painting, or good wainscot are no more unwholesome than bare wall . . ." (p. 119). While Mandeville has little faith in the ability of virtue to temper the desires, he points out that honor and the fear of ill-health can moderate the sensuous.

However, for the sake of argument, Mandeville supposes that the rich are enervated by their luxury and asks what effect this habit would have on the nation's strength. Are the rich expected to serve as common foot soldiers? Those grandees who are involved in military affairs are usually quite old and valued for their knowledge, not their strength. As for the rest of the rich, Mandeville asks, ". . . what have . . . people of any substance to do with war, but to pay taxes?" (p. 119).

The proponents of limiting luxury spending who see frugality as the means to national wealth had the powerful examples of Sparta and England's competitor Holland at their disposal. Sir William Temple's description of Dutch prosperity and the benefits of frugality were especially influential in the late seventeenth and early eighteenth centuries. Temple argued that wealth came from "the general industry and parsimony of a people"[46] and that the Dutch prospered because "they furnish luxury which they never practice, and traffic in pleasures which they never taste."[47]

While Temple takes care to describe the history of the Dutch and the geographical characteristics of their country, his belief that frugality is largely responsible for their wealth tends toward a moral interpretation of social life. Mandeville argues against this interpretation by emphasizing the particular historical and material factors that shaped Dutch frugality. He specifically assigns the reasons for Dutch frugality to necessity, not virtue.

> . . . The profuseness or frugality of a people in general, must always depend upon, and will . . . be ever proportioned to the fruitfulness

and product of the country, the number of inhabitants, and the taxes they are to bear. If anybody would refute what I have said, let him only prove from history, that there was ever in any country a national frugality without a national necessity.[48]

In the case of the Dutch this necessity was forced upon them by the long war they waged with the Spanish for their independence and the importance of maintaining their dikes. "Is it any wonder," says Mandeville, "that people under such circumstances, and loaded with greater taxes than any other nation, should be obliged to be saving?"[49] Mandeville argues that in areas where necessity did not oblige the Dutch to be frugal, as in the construction of their public buildings, they could be as profuse in their spending as any other nation.

The case of Sparta, which supposedly owed its strength to frugality and the absence of luxury, is quickly disposed of by Mandeville.[50] He simply denies that Spartan civilization was in any way praiseworthy. "But then their discipline was so rigid, and the manner of living so austere and void of all comfort, that the most temperate men among us would refuse to submit to the harshness of such uncouth laws."[51]

Mandeville's attack on frugality and his defense of luxury demand that he consider the basic analogy used by those who fear widespread luxury – the comparison of the economy of the individual or family with the economy of the state. In the earlier short discussions of the defense of luxury found in North and Barbon we have seen their rejection of this comparison. Mandeville continues this view when he states:

It is a received notion, that luxury is as destructive to the wealth of the whole body politic, as it is to that of every individual person who is guilty of it, and that a national frugality enriches a country in the same manner as that which is less general increases the estate of private families .... I cannot help dissenting from ... this point [pp. 108–109].

The same idea is specifically noted later in the *Fable*.

As this prudent economy, which some people call saving, is in private families the most certain method to increase an estate, so some imagine that whether a country be barren or fruitful, the same method, if generally pursued ... will have the same effect upon the whole nation .... This, I think, is an error [p. 182].

The refusal to equate the state with the individual is crucial to the attempt to separate virtue from the social world of commerce and is one of the strongest and most persistent themes in Mandeville's thought. He maintains that there is a public perspective which must be taken by the state and those interested in its development which is dependent upon principles different from, and perhaps antagonistic to, the principles inherited from traditional morality and applicable to the individual or family. The discussion of luxury and frugality afforded Mandeville one more opportunity to demonstrate that those measures appropriate to the sphere of the individual are inappropriate if applied to public policy. This effort is consistent with the overall objective of mercantilist thought "to make the state's purposes decisive in the economic sphere."[52]

If state policy aimed at promoting the virtue of frugality would not make a nation rich, what would? Mandeville begins by arguing that the real reasons for Dutch prosperity were "their political wisdom in postponing everything to merchandize and navigation, the unlimited liberty of conscience . . . and the unwearied application with which they have always made use of the most effectual means to encourage and increase trade in general."[53] And of all the means that were thought essential to trade, none was more widely discussed during the history of mercantilism than the doctrine of the balance of trade.

The aim of mercantilism was national power and national self-sufficiency. It demanded that the state be preeminent in the internal economic affairs of the country and therefore sought to destroy internal trade barriers, municipal autonomy, and local standards of weights and measures. In foreign affairs mercantilism's demand for independence meant intense international rivalries with other sovereign states. International trade in this period was thought to be a contest where the gains of one state necessarily meant losses in another. It was this belief that was at the basis of the doctrine of the balance of trade.

This doctrine rested on the attempt to maximize exports and limit imports so that the net balance of trade was to one's benefit. The balance could be computed two ways. One method demanded that the balance with each particular country should show the predominance of exports over imports. The other method of computation was concerned only that the total amount of goods exported was higher than the total amount of goods imported. The second method was more sophisticated in that it recognized the importance of the reexport trade. Though at least one economic historian maintains that both views were present throughout the history of mercantilism,[54] most commentators have found that the second view superseded the first in the last half of the seventeenth and first part of the eighteenth centuries.

The arguments in favor of the importance of a proper balance of trade were several. Those who attached primary importance to the possession of precious metals, bullionists, thought that a country like England, without mines to furnish it with gold or silver, could obtain these metals only by foreign trade. Because the mere bartering of goods contributed nothing to the nation's wealth (the supply of gold or silver), bullionists emphasized transactions where the total value of goods exported by England were more than the value of the goods obtained through imports. In such transactions the difference between the exports and imports would have to be made up by cash payments to England's advantage. The justifications and criticisms of the bullionist argument are irrelevant to this paper. It will suffice to say that gold and silver were considered necessary as the "sinews of war" and that many believed that internal economic activity was directly related to the amount of gold or silver in circulation.

In the view of many commentators the bullionist tendencies of mercantilism have been given undue prominence. Just as important to the mercantilist prohibitions on imports was the desire to protect and develop home industry. The common emphasis on the importation of raw materials and the exportation of finished products satisfied the requirements of the balance-of-trade doctrine because of the inexpensiveness of the raw materials and the higher value of the finished goods. Moreover, the process of converting raw materials to finished products provided employment for Englishmen. In fact, there were some Englishmen who found the chief justification of a proper balance of trade to be its implication that men in foreign countries were actually paying the wages of Englishmen, an idea sure to impress in this period of international competition.

In Comment L of the *Fable*, vol. 1, Mandeville presents the balance-of-trade argument, which computes the balance country by country and which argues for a national frugality. This argument holds that England receives no benefits from sending £1 million worth of goods to Turkey, for instance, even if it receives in return £1,200,000 worth of goods. In such a transaction goods have simply been bartered. But, if a frugal England consumes £600,000 or one-half as much and Turkey still needs the £1 million of goods as before, England would have to receive from Turkey £400,000 in money that would constitute profit.[55]

Mandeville counters this justification of frugality by pointing out that it dwells exclusively on the short-run advantages of trade and misunderstands the long-run interdependence of nations. Turkey would not continue to trade with England if she were always forced to pay cash and unable to exchange goods or sometimes receive cash from England.

> Buying is bartering, and no nation can buy goods of others that has none of her own to purchase them with . . . . We know that we could not continue long to purchase the goods of other nations, if they would not take our manufactures in payment for them; and why should we judge otherwise of other nations [p. 111].

Mandeville's awareness of the interdependence of nations in international trade provides him with a justification for the importation of luxury goods. If English merchants were unable to import, along with necessities, luxury goods – that is to exchange English goods for foreign luxury goods – overall English trade with countries that provide luxury goods would decline. Mandeville points out that merchants who send English goods to foreign countries in exchange for luxuries not only encourage English manufacturing but also help the shipping industry and increase custom revenues. F. B. Kaye is certainly correct when he observes that Mandeville, "wished to control the balance of trade, not by limiting imports, but by a stimulation of both exports and imports" (p. 111).

However, it should not be imagined that we have in Mandeville a systematic expression of the principles of international free trade or a total rejection of the balance-of-trade doctrine. Mandeville's position is consistent with the later stages of mercantilist thought.[56] Thus, instead of deemphasizing the role of government, Mandeville argues that those evils attributed to luxury spending are actually the result of the government not controlling closely enough its international trade and failing to maintain the proper balance.

> What is put to the account of luxury belongs to male-administration, and is the fault of bad politics. Every government ought to be thoroughly acquainted with, and steadfastly to pursue the interest of the country. Good politicians by dextrous management, laying heavy imposition on some goods, or totally prohibiting them, and lowering the duties on others, may always turn and divert the course of trade, which way they please . . . . above all they'll keep a watchful eye over the balance of trade in general, and never suffer that all foreign commodities together, that are imported in one year shall exceed in value what of their own growth or manufacture is in the same exported to others.[57]

The emphasis mercantilism placed on the maximization of exports had important repercussions on domestic labor policy. England's need to export as much as possible demanded, many thought, a large labor force. The revocation of the Edict of Nantes, with the resultant emigration of many skilled Huguenot workers, made it clear to many Englishmen that religious toleration was an important element of economic policy. Because England's ability to outsell her foreign competitors was also dependent upon the low price of her goods, mercantilist theory also sought to keep wages at subsistence levels. The emphasis on low wages was furthered by the belief that men were naturally slothful and tended to idleness unless forced by necessity to labor. The belief in the importance of low wages provides mercantilism with the paradox that the wealth of the state can be achieved through the poverty of its citizens. Eli Heckscher points out the difference between this view and that of laissez-faire: "Mercantilism was concerned with wealth simply as a basis for state power, while laissez-faire regarded it as valuable to the individual and worth striving for on that account."[58]

A close look at the domestic side of Mandeville's economic policy, which can be found clearly stated in his "Essay on Charity and Charity Schools" (1723), reveals its strictly mercantilist nature. The Charity Schools were not only part of the movement to reform manners, they were also a response to the problem of pauperism, "the one most important domestic problem of this age."[59] Not only were paupers not working to produce exportable goods for England, they were also responsible for draining the public treasury because of the poor-law payments made to them. The Charity Schools sought to educate the sons and daughters of the poor in the rudiments of reading, writing, and Christian morals, and then to place the students as maids or apprentices. It is in his opposition to these schools that Mandeville reveals his domestic labor doctrines.

Mandeville, always psychologically astute, begins by considering the motives behind the charity that enabled the schools to exist, reducing these motives to various forms of self-interest.

> Some come to it to save their credit, others to retrieve it. Others do it prudentially to increase their trade . . . . one motive above all . . . is to be carefully concealed, I mean the satisfaction there is in ruling over anything, and it is this chiefly that supports human nature in the tedious slavery of school-masters.[60]

Mandeville is no more kind in his discussion of the specific justifications given for the Charity Schools. To the argument that the schools taught children how to read the word of God and would thereby improve their morality, Mandeville replied that "vice in general is no where more predominant than where arts and science flourish, ignorance is . . . counted to be the mother of devotion, and it is certain that we shall find innocence and honesty no where more general than among the most illiterate, the poor silly country people" (p. 269).

However, because the moving force behind the Charity Schools was economic, to train the children of the poor to be productive, Mandeville was led to consider the economic position and importance of the poor. According to Mandeville, instead of increasing productivity, the schools actually promoted idleness. "Every hour those of poor people spend at their books," he argued, "is so much time lost to the society. Going to school in comparison to working is idleness" (p. 288). Not only did the Charity Schools detract from the present productive capacity of the nation, they also endangered its future capacity for production, for "the longer boys continue in this easy sort of life, the more unfit they'll be when grown up for downright labour, both as to strength and inclination" (p. 288). The children educated in these schools will expect to find positions for themselves that will employ their ability to read and write, and they will look down upon mere common labor. Moreover, education is incompatible with the labor of the poor because it opens new possibilities to the poor, which cause them to be dissatisfied with their social position. "It is requisite," states Mandeville, "that great numbers of them should be ignorant as well as poor, knowledge both enlarges and multiplies our desires, and the fewer things a man wishes for, the more easily his necessities may be supplied" (pp. 287–288).

In this last quotation it can be seen that Mandeville had before him the great secret of the industrial revolution and laissez-faire economics – the creation of mass markets through the multiplication of desires.[61] Yet, because he lived in and believed in a mercantile economy, he could only envision a society based on luxury spending by the rich and hard work by the ignorant poor. Categorically Mandeville states that "the surest wealth consists in a multitude of laborious poor . . ."[62] This vast class of laboring poor is needed because "the plenty and cheapness of provisions depends in a great measure on the price and value that is set upon labour" (p. 287). And if labor can be kept cheap "we must infallibly out-sell our neighbors" (p. 286). It is no wonder that Mandeville counsels "a wise legislature [to] cultivate the breed of them with all imaginable care" (p. 287).

Finally, Mandeville objects that the trades for which the Charity Schools are training young men are already overflowing and that therefore the schools are meddling with the proper balance set by supply and demand. "This proportion as to numbers in every trade finds itself, and is never better kept than when no body meddles or interferes" (p. 300). Just as important, the schools violate the integrity of this highly stratified class society by placing the children of the poor in positions above their station and displacing the sons of honest shopkeepers who rightly deserve these positions (p. 298). One of Mandeville's allies in the attack on Charity Schools, John Trenchard, a co-author of *Cato's Letters*, argued in the same way that the schools "take the lowest dregs of the people from the plough and labour, to make them tradesmen and by consequence drive the children of tradesmen to the plough, to bed, to rob, or to starve."[63] Instead of taking the jobs of their betters, Mandeville would have the idle poor put to work by the government draining lands, building canals, making rivers navigable, and improving the roads.

The theories of labor found in Mandeville underline the ways in which his economic doctrines are different from the laissez-faire ideas that will become popular later in the century. In his classic work on the position of the laborer in mercantile society, Edgar Furniss states that "it is not true of mercantile theory, as it is of utilitarian, that the goal of national endeavor is the economic prosperity of the individual citizens."[64] On a more general level, as another scholar has observed, this belief illustrates that "the coincidence of public and private advantage is not yet part of intellectual equipment."[65] In the *Wealth of Nations* Adam Smith is at pains to establish just this coincidence and to argue that a prosperity which leaves the mass of citizens in poverty is not to the benefit of the nation.

> But what improves the circumstances of the greater part can never be regarded as an inconveniency to the whole. No society can surely be flourishing and happy, of which the greater part of the members are poor and miserable.[66]

Were it not for our understanding that mercantilists typically believed that the majority must be kept in poverty so that the whole might be rich, this quotation from Smith would sound as if it were written directly against Mandeville.

Mandeville's famous phrase "private vices, public virtues" at first seems to indicate that he identified, perhaps was even the first explicitly to identify, public and private advantage. Surely this is the interpretation given that phrase by those who see Mandeville as an early or even the first laissez-faire economist.[67] A closer analysis, however, reveals that "private vices, public virtues" refers exclusively to the prodigality of the high-born and the avarice of the merchant. We find in Mandeville the picture of a strictly differentiated class-structured society, which depends for its prosperity on the poverty of the vast majority of the population. Mandeville opposed the upward mobility of this class and did not extend to the laboring poor his pyschological insights into the power of avarice or vanity to motivate economic activity. Only the threat of starvation keeps the poor from idleness.

While the demand for low wages was typical of mercantile thought, there were some in this period who saw, years before Adam Smith, the economic benefits of high wages. In 1690 Josiah Child explicitly argued that high wages were productive and a sign of prosperity. He noted that the Dutch paid higher wages than the English and that this did not adversely affect their trade. Good laws and a large population brought wealth to a nation, while low wages only drove men to leave England and settle in countries which paid higher wages. He concluded that "wherever wages are high, universally throughout the whole world, it is an infallible evidence of the riches of that country; and wherever wages for labour runs low, it is a proof of the poverty of that place."[68] Other justifications for higher wages can also be found in the works of Carey and North.[69]

Mandeville's criticism of the Charity Schools occasioned a spate of pamphlets answering his charges. Most of the schools' defenders did not disagree that the poor must always remain poor, but argued simply that the religious education of the schools taught submission, obedience, and hard work.[70] Isaac Watts, who suggested that perhaps the schools would benefit if manual labor were to occupy part of the day, voiced the typical view when he said that ". . . God has wisely ordained . . . that . . . there shall be some rich, and some poor. . . . Nor is it possible to alter this constitution of things. . . ."[71]

There are, however, at least two examples of men who responded to Mandeville by questioning his views that the poor had to remain in the station in which they were born. William Hendley, a high church divine, suggested that the poor had an equal right to some of the conveniences and comforts of life hitherto reserved only for the rich. "It is," he said, "both unjust and unnatural to make the poor always slaves to the rich, and exclude them and their children forever from bettering their fortunes in the world."[72] Instead of seeing the low wages of agricultural workers as good policy, Hendley believed it showed that the rural population was too large and would benefit from some of its members entering the trades.

Like Hendley, George Bluett, one of the few laymen to enter the controversy, argued that the low wages paid to farm workers showed that area to be overstocked.[73]    The kingdom would benefit, according to Bluett, if farm laborers who earned 8 pence a day became tradesmen who earned 16 pence a day. Bluett specifically argued against the notion that the prosperity of society depended upon great numbers of poor and ignorant laborers. The effect of greater plenty would be that men would be paid more for performing the same menial tasks they now performed for low wages. Nor was it necessary to worry about tasks not being performed if wages rose. If, for example, fewer men became chimney sweeps the law of supply and demand would raise the wages of chimney sweeps until more men were attracted to that job. Even more impressive was Bluett's understanding that the key to stimulating trade and prosperity was to increase the wants and desires of all classes of men.

Thus, not only are Mandeville's economic doctrines on the position of the laborer standard mercantilist fare, they are typical in an age in which some men had rejected the necessity of keeping wages low.

Mandeville's attitude toward the laboring poor also betrays the limits of his individualism. Many writers, Albert Schatz especially, have sought to find in Mandeville the origins of economic individualism.[74] And there is little doubt that Mandeville's analysis of the nonlaboring classes is based on unmasking and justifying the individual's desire for self-aggrandizement. This segment of society is populated by pleasure-seeking, atomistic individuals whose desire for gain is used by the government in its policies. But, Mandeville's economic individualism does not extend to the laboring poor, whom he treats as a class lacking in the desire for material improvement and individual assertion. Edgar Furniss's explanation of the nonindividualistic policy of mercantilism toward the laboring poor could as easily be applied to Mandeville.

The fact that the laboring population was viewed as a *class* [emphasis his] and dealt with as a class shows that individualist concepts of society did not embrace them. As a class they were to be patronized by the government, as a class coerced, disciplined, punished, when patronage failed to awaken the expected response. Much was said of their duties and their station in life, little or nothing of their opportunities for advancement in the social scale; few were the proposals to throw them upon their own resources as individuals, many those which advocated comprehensive government action to control their conduct as a group.[75]

It is also important to understand that, however provocative Mandeville's formulation of economic individualism was (so far as it went), this individualism was throughout mercantilist and not, as some would have it, a decisive step taken by Mandeville toward laissez-faire economics. Jacob Viner, for instance, concludes that "The concept of the economic man, instead of being, as is often alleged, an invention of the nineteenth century classical school, was an important element in mercantilist thought."[76] Economic self-interest was mercantilism's contribution to the nonmoral explanation of the social world also sought by Jansenism and skepticism.

Though mercantilism and laissez-faire have in common the ideal of an economic man, the two systems differ in the amount of freedom of action granted to individuals in the pursuit of their economic self-interest. As is well known, the mercantilist often finds that private interest contradicts the public good so that a powerful state is necessary to establish an artificial order between the individual and society, while the proponents of laissez-faire believe that a natural harmony exists between the individual's economic self-assertions and the welfare of society. The relationship between private vice and public virtue is clearly at the heart of this problem. Since Mandeville, as Francis Hutcheson pointed out, connected these two with only a comma, his position is far from obvious.[77]

There is no greater temptation in historical research than to try to find in men of ages past our own ideas and prejudices. The discovery that our own beliefs have a long – the longer the better – and glorious history is at least one way of enhancing their legitimacy. Late seventeenth- and early eighteenth-century economic history has suffered particularly from this problem as writers search to find precursors to Adam Smith and the doctrines of laissez-faire. As T. E. Gregory has stated:

> No period in English economic history has suffered more from the tendency of subjecting facts to a preconceived notion than has the

Restoration period. Regarded by some as the period of neo-mercantilism, more recently by others as the period of incipient capitalism, the interrelation of ideas has not been analyzed as an end in itself before the final judgment has been passed.[78]

This tendency, it seems to me, has been particularly strong in Mandeville scholarship, especially in the attempt to find in his work the idea of an order which naturally and spontaneously reconciles individual self-love with the public good. Mandeville states specifically in the preface to the *Fable* "that those very vices of every particular person by *skilful Management*, were made subservient to the grandeur and worldly happiness of the whole,"[79] and then repeats himself in the last words of the *Fable* by stating "that private vices by the *dextrous management of a skillful politician*, may be turned into public benefits."[80] In the *Vindication of the Book* attached to the end of the third edition of the *Fable* in 1723, he states explicitly:

> I am sorry if the words private vices, public benefits have ever given offense to a well-meaning man. The mystery of them is soon unfolded ⸱ ᐧhen once they are rightly understood; but no man of sincerity will question the innocence of them, that has read the last paragraph, when I take leave of the reader, and conclude with repeating the seeming paradox the substance of which is advanced in the title page; *that private vices by the dextrous management of a skillful politician may be turned into public benefits.*[81]

Mandeville continues to insist upon this interpretation of his paradox in 1732, when in his reply to Berkeley he states "that luxury and vices of man, *under the regulation and restrictions* laid down in the *Fable of the Bees*, are ... inseparable from the earthly felicity of civil society."[82] The ideas found in these quotations are consistent with mercantilism's recognition of man's egoism and its attempt to use this passion to increase the economic power of the nation through a discipline or "skillful management" enforced by the government.

The spontaneous reconciliation of economic interests supposes the benevolence of nature. This strain of thought is basic to the ideas of Mandeville's opponent, Shaftesbury; one of Mandeville's most persistent detractors, Hutcheson; and is found later in the century in both Hume and Smith. In Mandeville, on the contrary, one searches in vain for this turn of mind. Instead, there is throughout Mandeville's work the motif of art and artifice. Rather than exalting the natural and spontaneous he is at pains to show that its influence is slight. "The part, which nature contributed toward the skill and patience of every single person ... was very inconsiderable .... The difference between the works of art, and those of nature, is so immense, that it is impossible not to know them asunder."[83] While groups of animals may live according to the fixed and unalterable laws of nature, men "whose societies cannot exist without the concurrence of human wisdom" (p. 187) need art and experience. "Nature," Mandeville says, "has given us nothing but the ore, which she has hid in the bowels of the earth" (p. 188). And in the last dialogue in the *Fable*, vol. 2, Mandeville states that his purpose was "to demonstrate . . . that the good qualities men compliment our nature and the whole species with, are the result of art and education" (p. 306).

When applied to politics, Mandeville's ideas emphasizing the extreme egoism of man, the denigration of nature, and the necessity of artifice result in his insistence on the importance of government. It is hardly possible to hold a more exalted view of government than to believe, as Mandeville does, that "laws and governments are to the political bodies of civil societies, what the vital spirits and life itself are to the natural bodies of animated creatures"[84] or to hold that "to be a consummate statesman, is the highest qualification human nature is capable of possessing."[85] It is clear that Mandeville did not hold that there was a natural harmony among men because of an innate, other-regarding principle, which seems to be the case with Shaftesbury and Hutcheson, for example. It should now also be clear that Mandeville did not believe in a spontaneous order arising out of the self-regarding actions of men.[86] On the contrary, the egoism of man demanded what seems to be continual governmental activity. Thus,

> the regulations only, that are required to defeat and prevent all the machinations and contrivances, that avarice and envy may put man upon to the detriment of his neighbour are almost infinite. Would you be convinced of these truths, do but employ yourself . . . in surveying and . . . examining . . . all the laws, prohibitions, ordinances and restrictions, that have been found absolutely necessary . . . . you will find the number of clauses and provisos, to govern a large flourishing city well, to be prodigious beyond imagination; and yet every one of them tending to the same purpose, the curbing, restraining and disappointing the inordinate passions and hurtful frailities of man.[87]

In economics specifically the whole notion of a balance of trade is impossible unless one assumes a government ready to control the amount of goods imported and exported. Therefore, Mandeville suggests that "Good politicians by dextrous management, laying heavy impositions on some goods, or totally prohibiting them, and lowering the duties on others, may also turn and divert the course of trade which way they please."[88]

Moreover, there is not in Mandeville any notion of the theoretical limitation of government activity. His specific proposals, for example, to end government control over luxury goods or for religious toleration are quite common to mercantilists of his age. So far is Mandeville from setting systematic boundaries to government activity that he can state: "The great business in general of a politician is to promote, and, if he can, reward all good and useful actions on the one hand; and on the other, to punish, or at least discourage, everything that is destructive or hurtful to society."[89]

No one as aware of man's frailities as Mandeville could possibly ground his desire for effective governmental regulation on the presence in government of virtuous men. To expect only virtuous men to be in government, he says, "is to betray great ignorance in human affairs."[90] But though he is aware of the tendency of selfish men to misuse their office, there are checks on such men which make it possible to reconcile an active view of government with a pessimistic view of the motives of the men in government. Not surprisingly Mandeville has some notions of checks within the government, so that, for example, the parliament's power over a minister will contribute to his honesty. Another check, more characteristic of Mandeville's thought, can be found in man's selfish desire to be well thought of by others – his pride. Because men desire to maintain their reputations they will carry out their duties properly.

Mandeville's sensitivity to the long and slow process by which political and economic institutions evolve also provides him with reason to believe that government can operate effectively. Society does not depend upon the genius of individual men to make good laws but on the experience of many generations. Thus, Mandeville argues that the "clauses and provisos" which regulate society are not "the work of one man, or of one generation; the greatest part of them are the product, the joynt labour of several ages."[91] This long period of evolution does not make regulation less necessary; rather, it contributes to making management more artful and the rules of government more effective.

The last safeguard proposed by Mandeville to ensure the proper functioning of government is uncannily prescient, since it foresees the growth of modern bureaucracy. He proposes that the division of labor which enables ordinary men to supply society's economic needs could also be supplied to government. The division of labor would not only simplify the tasks that must be performed by government, it would also increase each government employee's sense of responsibility. He argues that

> by careful limitations of every man's power, and judicious cheques upon everybody's trust, every officer's fidelity may be placed in so clear a light, that, the moment he forfeits it, he must be detected . . . by these arts . . . . the weightiest affairs . . . may be managed with safety . . . by ordinary men, whose highest good is wealth and pleasure.[92]

These are not the words of a laissez-faire philosopher denigrating government and its bureaucracy; they are, instead, a prescription by a man who sees the need for government regulation and who is attempting to devise a formula that will allow men of middling capacities to carry out the important functions of government.

Mandeville's comments on government are perfectly consistent with his rejection of the moral interpretation of society. Just as he has sought nonmoral explanations for the evolution of society and its ability to provide men with economic goods and services, he has here gone so far as to banish virtue from our consideration of government. In his *Free Thoughts on Religion, the Church, and National Happiness* (1720), he has explicitly argued that while the traditional criteria of moral virtue may be applicable to the consideration of men as individuals, they are inappropriate to the consideration of men from the perspective of their public duties.

> . . . all men ought to be considered two different ways.
>
> First as to their occupation . . . and here we chiefly mind the usefulness and dignity of the calling, their capacities . . . . In this view we have no regard for the persons themselves but only the benefit they may be to the public . . . .
>
> Secondly, every person is to be considered as an entire individual, a wonderful machine, endowed with thought and will . . . .[93]

And in *A Modest Defense of Publick Stews* (p. 68) he argues that "It is the grossest absurdity, and a perfect contradiction in terms, to assert that a government may not commit evil that a good may come of it." In the same way that Mandeville has drawn strictly the lines between virtue and commerce, he has here just as strictly separated virtue and government.

# Chapter 5 Mandeville and His Critics

We have found in the work of Bernard Mandeville a total acceptance of the new commercial world of the early eighteenth century. Yet we have seen that Mandeville accepted the world of commerce without trying to integrate it into the moral world. Instead, he maintained throughout his work that commercial activity was inconsistent with the practice of virtue. Mandeville constructed his apology by arguing that the alternative to a commercial world based on self-interest, i.e., a virtuous society based on public-spiritedness, was merely a "romantik fancy." While Mandeville maintained the tension between virtue and commerce and obviously enjoyed putting men into the position of having to choose one or the other, other men found this position uncomfortable and, in their responses to Mandeville, sought a way out of the dilemma. Some writers, seemingly unaware of the threat of commerce to their traditional beliefs, simply restated Christian precepts. Still other traditionalists took Mandeville on his own terms and tried to show that Christian morality and some level of commercial prosperity were perfectly compatible. More interesting are those like Archibald Campbell and Francis Hutcheson, who tried to rescue virtue by shifting its basis from Christian self-denial to more utilitarian considerations. And, finally, there is David Hume's argument that commerce so far from being incompatible with virtue was actually a force that promoted it.

Those moralists who responded to Mandeville objected first of all to the pyrrhonism contained in his argument that "moral virtues are the political offspring which flattery begot upon pride."[1] Because of the close connection in this period between moral thought and psychology, this problem in its largest sense concerned the constitution of man. In order to counter Mandeville's skepticism and his belief in pervasive selfishness, his opponents either asserted the reality, strength, and ability of reason to guide men or the reality and strength of the social passions to move men prior to any considerations of narrow self-interest. In both cases it was necessary to argue against Mandeville's belief that, because pleasure accompanied many seemingly virtuous acts, those acts were undertaken in order to gain pleasure and were, therefore, not virtuous at all.[2] Both alternatives envisaged a harmonious society rather than one based on egoism and antagonistic relationships.

The second problem that faced writers who argued with Mandeville, and the one that is more specifically germane to social thought and this book was the relationship between a moral psychology that upheld virtue and the problem of psychologically motivating men to provide economic goods and services to society. To what extent was the virtue of public-spiritedness compatible with a commercial society based on economic self-interest? Most often this problem is discussed in the context of the debate over luxury, for in the early eighteenth century it was luxury that came to stand for those private desires and private satisfactions, usually grounded in matters of money, that seemed to threaten public-spiritedness and the social fabric. We will see that although some of the men who responded to Mandeville were moved to redefine virtue so that it was more consistent with the passions and to consider luxury in such a way that it was compatible with great wealth, few, if any (apart from Hume), were able to view without worry the effects of unlimited economic self-aggrandizement on the soul of the individual and the constitution of society.

A simple and straightforward rejection of "free thinking" because of its social consequences can be found in Edmund Gibson, the bishop of London. He shared the view of the moral reformers that an "unprecedented licentiousness" was spreading throughout England, and in order to help combat this infidelity he wrote a pastoral letter in 1726 urging the magistrates to suppress works which treated revealed religion in a ludicrous manner.[3] The objects of his attack were the new ideas in which "Publick Stews have been openly vindicated and private vices recommended to the protection of government as public benefits,"[4] obvious references to Mandeville. Just as destructive, according to Gibson, were the ideas that had "shown a great zeal for natural religion in opposition to revealed" (p. 3). Against the view of both Mandeville and Shaftesbury he upheld the necessity of self-denial to restrain "the irregular appetites of mankind" (p. 10).

The view that Mandeville had sought "to make men easy in their vices" (p. 2), as Gibson put it, to provide an apology for all vicious actions, was commonly charged against him. Bishop Berkeley, for example, argued that he justified drunkenness and robbery among other evil actions, and John Thorold wondered how the government could punish anyone if it was thought that vicious actions led to the public good.[5] It was even believed that Mandeville defended drunkenness because he was in the pay of the distillers.[6] Clearly this attitude misunderstood the major thrust of Mandeville's ideas. Mandeville's aim was primarily to

justify as public benefits those acts that were private vices only according to the public-spirited or rigorist view of morality. He wanted to
show that avaricious, vain, self-interested acts which contravened the
standards of civic humanism or were vicious by rigorist standards of
morality were nevertheless necessary to commercial society. He was
perfectly capable of advocating, indeed his social thought demanded,
that acts such as drunkenness or robbery be punished insofar as they
impaired the productive capacities of society.[7]

John Thorold in the style of a traditionalist also objected to
Mandeville's reduction of moral rules to the cunning use of pride by
politicians and asserted that the ideas of right and wrong were grafted
onto the hearts of men at the fall. He believed that men were not merely
self-interested, passion-dominated creatures who could act properly
only if flattered. Men were, he thought, capable of acting through "sentiments of duty and obedience . . . inspired by a just sense of infinite
mercy, and boundless loving kindness of our Creator's will."[8] Thorold
objected to Mandeville's unsympathetic psychological analysis of men
of good breeding and the clergy, which suggested that these men simply
concealed their baser passions, and he was outraged at Mandeville's
argument that the Christian martyrs stood fast in their beliefs simply
because of their pride. Taken together Mandeville's ideas seemed to
Thorold to be those of a Goth or Vandal bent on destroying civilization.

More interesting is Thorold's reaction to the contradiction between
virtue and commerce. The notion that frugality was unnecessary for a
trading nation Thorold could only dismiss "with just scorn and
derision." But, above all, in a discussion on the relationship between
contentment and industry Thorold wanted to rescue virtue, which
should result in contentment, from Mandeville's charge that it is impossible in a wealthy commercial society. Thus, Thorold stated, "All I
insist upon amounts to this, that content and industry are not incompatible. I mean a man may make a competent provision for himself and
family, and yet . . . not be a stranger to content of mind" (p. 27). Yet, a
page earlier Thorold seemed inadvertently to have given the argument
to Mandeville when he said of the contented man that "he leaves it to
more ambitious heads, and more craving appetites to bustle in the
world; and to sacrifice their repose; and too often their conscience to
sordid interest" (p. 26). It seemed that in spite of himself Thorold had
exactly recognized the alternative upon which Mandeville insisted. Virtue and contentment, if consistent with a "competent provision," were
inconsistent with a wealthy and powerful mercantile state which
demanded ambitious men of "craving appetites." Thorold remained
certain that the true end of man was in "executing the commands of his
Maker" and that the "worldly-minded wretch, ever heaping up, and
ever thirsting after riches" (p. 26), destroyed himself and society.

The distinction found in Thorold between a "competent provision" and the ambitious and craving appetites of a "worldly-minded wretch" seems akin to John Dennis's attempt to use the idea of the golden mean to distinguish between wealth and luxury.[9] Dennis, a staunch defender of the 1688 revolution, argued along the lines we have come to associate with the tradition of civic humanism. He quoted with approval Algernon Sidney's *Discourse Concerning Government* and Machiavelli's *Discourses.* And like "so great a politician as Machiavelli" (p. 13), he believed in the necessity of a strong established religion, especially in a free country. A civil religion was important, according to Dennis, because it brought to life the contract between the prince and the people. This contract was based on the oaths sworn by both parties, the one to obey and the other to rule within the law. If religion fell into disrepute these oaths would lose their binding power.

The necessity of a widespread awareness of public responsibility was particularly crucial to Dennis because he shared the general belief in England's rampant corruption. "The people of Great Britain," he said, "were never so divided as they are at present . . . for not only the whole body of the nation is divided into Whig and Tory, but Whigs are divided against Whigs and Tories against Tories,.and the division has got into private families, where the father is divided against the son, and the husband against the wife" (p. 24). Of all the vices that were responsible for the decline in public concern and England's sad plight, none seemed to have done more harm than the spread of and desire for luxury.

Mandeville's argument that luxury was a meaningless concept was part of his attempt to justify unlimited economic self-aggrandizement. Because Dennis believed that economic self-interest unchecked could undermine concern for the public, he was concerned to give a clear meaning to luxury and to distinguish legitimate interest in a "competent provision" from the unlimited pursuit of riches. He argued that the idea of a golden mean separated the proper from the improper concern for economic self-interest. Just as men's reason was capable of understanding the difference between eating and drinking too little and too much, and then reaching the mean, which was eating enough to support life, it was able to apprehend the amount of concern for material possession that was appropriate to life and society.

Having defended the reality of luxury, Dennis was able to discuss its ill effects. He concurred with the common complaint that widespread luxury was incompatible with military strength because it weakened the physical constitution of man. More interesting was his view of the effect of luxury when it was identified with avarice and vanity.

When there is a general contention who shall out do and outshine his neighbor in the pomp and splendor of it: in the pomp and splendor of buildings, furniture, gardens, apparel, equipage, and sumptuous table ... then riches, the food and support of luxury, are fought for with insatiable avarice, and to obtain them, the most solemn obligations are infringed, the most sacred truths violated [p. 27].

While Mandeville argued that luxury was unimportant, even helpful, as long as the administration of government remained wise, Dennis replied that it was precisely the wise administration of government that was undermined when luxury, the concern to outshine one's neighbor in "pomp and splendor," permeated society (pp. 74–75).

The link between civic humanism and the Charity Schools can clearly be seen in Dennis. He criticized Mandeville not only for writing an apology for vice which destroyed the bonds between the individual and society needed in a free country, but also for attacking one method of restoring public virtue – the Charity Schools. Like most who defended the schools, Dennis stressed the importance of their teaching godly discipline and humility to the poor and, by teaching the children of the poor to read Scripture by themselves, their ability to protect the poor from the orations of Jacobites. It is clear that for Dennis (though not for all of the schools' defenders) the children of the poor are educated so that they can undertake their civic reponsibilities.

The doctrine of "private vices, public virtues" was incomprehensible to Dennis. To him it was axiomatic that "vice is always attended by corruption" (p. 13). But surely he was correct historically when he stated that Mandeville's ideas "contradict the sense of mankind in all preceeding ages .... So strange an assertion makes all writers of politics, from Plato to Machiavelli, contemptible ignorant fools ..." (pp. 12–13).

While Dennis is interesting because he reflects and participates in the tradition opposed to Mandeville's, another commentator on the *Fable of the Bees*, George Bluett, first attracts our attention because of his awareness of Mandeville's tradition.[10] He noted Mandeville's use of the French moralists Montaigne, La Rochefoucauld, Jacques Esprit, and Pierre Bayle, whom he accused Mandeville of following blindly. And in the beginning of his pamphlet he sought to turn the tables on Mandeville by using a quotation from La Rochefoucauld to describe Mandeville's work.

That as wicked as men are, they never dare to profess themselves enemies to virtue; and when they have to persecute it, they either pretend not to think it real, or forge some faults and lay it to its charge.[11]

Though Bluett was concerned with the pyrrhonism found in Mandeville's work and with defending the importance of a civil religion, it was a discussion of luxury that occupied most of the book. Here again luxury was the specific issue that contained the larger question of the relationship between virtue and commerce. While Bluett continued to use the idea of luxury, and was therefore ready at some point to condemn economic aggrandizement, his formulation of it went further than either Thorold or Dennis in accepting the commercial world.

Bluett had to define luxury so that it could apply to some cases that could be seen as immoral, but at the same time not define it so widely that it might characterize and condemn too much of the commercial world. Bluett set out immediately to justify superfluities and conveniences. Because no one part of the earth produced all the things that could be found on the earth as a whole, men learned to exchange whatever they had in abundance for what they needed. Since most nations had the bare necessities for life, trade was generally only for superfluities. In fact, it was the mark of a successful trading nation that it gathered as many non-necessary products as possible. "Public wealth," he said, "may be said to consist in the greatest plenty of ornaments" (p. 3). The accumulation of these "ornaments" constituted neither a vice nor a public disadvantage. Almost echoing Mandeville, he asked, "What greater immorality is there in the work of the finest chizel, or the nicest plane, than in that of an ax or a saw . . .?" (p. 36). The accumulation of ornaments and improvements was the very purpose of trade, sanctioned by God who created a world in which trade was necessary. God gave to man the earth for man's use. "All the fruits of the earth were designed for the service of man, and his skill and capacity in the improvement of them were given him by nature, to make his present being easy and agreeable to him, in everything, which does not interfere with the happiness of a future one" (pp. 36–37).

Bluett took Mandeville's position to be that the general practice of virtue was inconsistent with the accumulation of these ornaments and the improvement of conveniences. Bluett argued in response that if those who were employed by dishonesty – policemen, jailers, lawyers, etc. – were no longer needed, they could find work improving the soil or its products. The real wealth of the country would, according to Bluett, increase and not decrease with virtue. However, the reconciliation of virtue and commerce had been accomplished in this case by using the narrow conception of vice as law-breaking. Mandeville's point, however, was to show that the accumulation of luxury depended upon the free play of man's egoism, which was condemned by traditional standards of virtue that demanded public-spiritedness and rationality.

Though Bluett defended society's wealth as consistent with virtue he was still traditional enough to stop short of abandoning the idea that there was a particular vice called luxury. He found this vice in an "excess of ease and pleasure . . . or in greater expense than is proportioned to peoples circumstances and fortunes . . ." (p. 37). He repeated the common notion that luxury weakened a people and used the example of Spain where, he maintained, the discovery of gold and silver in the new world had made the people grow slow and idle. The counter example of the Dutch provided him with a model of people made rich by frugality.

It seems at first glance that Bluett's defense of increasing prosperity was inconsistent with the traditional idea that luxury caused weakness. But there was a way in which they could be reconciled. First, in Bluett's formulation what was and was not luxury varied with one's station in life. If the poor were to acquire too much wealth they would stop working. The wealth of the aristocracy, on the other hand, provided an identification with the country and caused them to act in ways that benefited the public. However, when their concern for ornaments became too great their identification with the country could be broken. In both cases luxury seemed to begin where the amount of wealth in each person's possession undermined the function he was to play in society.

The second test that could detect luxurious spending was the balance of trade. The idea of luxury was so closely tied to the balance of trade that Bluett refused to believe that Mandeville was serious when he argued that imports should never exceed exports. In Bluett's view, which was typical of the time, the necessary effect of any apology for luxury must be the destruction of the balance of trade by increasing the amount spent on imports.

While Bluett still retained the idea of the reality of luxury, he did so only after granting a good deal to Mandeville. The view that luxury was relative to the wealth of each station, and that the rich could live as pleasantly as they pleased so long as they could pay for it, was not unique to Bluett, but can also be found in the work of Bishop Berkeley.

Berkeley was, of course, morally incensed at Mandeville's paradox because it seemed to him to be an apology for such vices as drunkenness, gambling, robbery, and philandering.[12] The free thinker created by Berkeley to argue Mandeville's position in the dialogue entitled *Alciphron* justified these acts on the grounds that they gave employment to many tradesmen. Though Berkeley was acutely aware that increased aggregate demand provided employment, he could not accept Mandeville's conclusion that the vices of men were needed for that purpose. He argued that while a vicious man could consume much in a short time his vices would lead him to an early death. A virtuous man, however, would consume over a long and healthy life and, in the long run, consume more than a rake. Using the most common analogy in economic discussions, Berkeley maintained that a kingdom, just like a private family, did not prosper from vice. As the vices in the kingdom increased, Berkeley argued, the number of people would decrease, which would increase the cost of labor and the cost of finished products, and this would hurt the balance of trade. Virtuousness and the balance of trade complement one another.

Though Berkeley countered Mandeville's free thinking by arguing that the true end of mankind was not wealth, he was concerned about the economic conditions in Ireland, especially the problem of widespread unemployment. Though Berkeley found luxury morally suspect he, like Mandeville, looked to the spending of the wealthy to support employment among the lower orders. In *Alciphron* he linked luxury to station and maintained that expenditures in proportion to fortune, without foolish ostentation, were not luxury.[13] This position was stated more explicitly a few years later in Berkeley's most specifically economic work *The Querist* (1735–36–37).[14] Here he not only justified but actually pleaded with the Irish nobility to spend more lavishly.

394. Whether the most indolent would be fond of idleness, if they regarded it as the sure road to hard labour?

395. Whether the industry of the lower part of our people doth not much depend on the expense of the upper?

396. What would be the consequence if our gentry affected to distinguish themselves by fine houses rather than fine clothes?

397. Whether any people in Europe are so meanly provided with houses and furniture, in proportion to their incomes, as the men of estates in Ireland?

398. Whether building would not peculiarly encourage all other arts in this kingdom?

399. Whether smiths, masons, bricklayers, plasterers, carpenters, joiners, tilers, plumbers, and glaziers would not all find employment if the humour of building prevailed?

400. Whether the ornaments and furniture of a good house do not employ a number of all sorts of artificers, in iron, wood, marble, brass, pewter, copper, wool, flax, and divers other materials?

401. Whether in buildings and gardens a great number of day-labourers do not find employment?

402. Whether by these means much of that sustenance and wealth of this nation which now goes to foreigners would not be kept at home, and nourish and circulate among our own people?

403. Whether, as industry produced good living, the number of hands and mouths would not be increased; and in proportion thereunto, whether there would not be every day more occasion for agriculture? And whether this article alone would not employ a world of people?

404. Whether such management would not equally provide for the magnificence of the rich, and the necessities of the poor?[15]

Mandeville's discussion of luxury was offensive to the

eighteenth-century mind because it removed the question of luxury from any moral considerations. The problem faced by Mandeville's critics was to find a definition of luxury that allowed for the liberal spending of the wealthy, an economic necessity according to mercantilism, but within a framework of moral rules. The view that luxury was spending above one's means had the benefit of being specific enough to apply to the situation of each individual as well as to counter Mandeville's argument that luxury was too ambiguous a term to be used in social analysis, while at the same time it legitimized the wealth and even the ostentation of the well-to-do. However, the importance attached to the injunction against spending over one's fortune attested to the uneasiness on the part of many about the commercial world's tendency to raise individual desires and appetites in ways that could lead men to violate their responsibilities to others and to the public. The paradigmatic examples of such violations were a man spending so much gambling that he could no longer provide for his dependents, and a man betraying his country for a price.

Thus, Berkeley and the other traditional Christian moralists who criticized Mandeville were able to accept luxury spending by the rich so long as it was within their means. But, because they held more or less closely to moral standards, that demanded reason or self-denial, they were not able to counter directly Mandeville's arguments about the motivations of men needed in commercial society. It is in the Scottish School, as one might expect, that we find the fullest and most interesting criticism of Mandeville. Because these writers began with a new definition of virtue, they were able to consider self-interest in such a way that it was consistent with virtue, and thereby moved to a self-conscious reconciliation of virtue and the necessities of a commercial society.

One of the earliest utilitarian critiques of Mandeville was put forward by Archibald Campbell.[16] He began by stating that all men have implanted in their nature by God the principle of self-love, which moved men not only to preserve themselves, but also to live well. This nature included not only the desire to have companions, but to be well liked and esteemed by those companions. By stressing the origins of self-love in God and by defining self-love to cover much more than simple self-preservation, Campbell had changed pleasure seeking from a mere psychological fact to a moral fact.

The first task of Campbell in his discussion of luxury was to counter Mandeville's claim that luxury was either everything or nothing at all. He wanted to abate the severe definition of luxury, which included all the improvements man had made, and yet still maintain a standard that made it possible to identify some things as luxury. Like Bluett, Campbell seemed to move many more goods outside the purview of luxury than he moved into this sphere. Because God had given men senses and made the world delightful there was, according to Campbell, no sin or luxury in the enjoyment of these pleasures. In the same way, because our powers to improve the world were God's creation, there was no necessary luxury in artfully providing life with more conveniences. Thus, Campbell concluded

> That the duties of nature having so settled the constitution of things, that it is impossible for us not to perceive numberless other satisfactions, besides those that arise from such objects as are absolutely necessary to keep us alive; we may all cheerfully indulge to ourselves those gratifications without the least degree of vice and luxury [p.120].

Even if men were motivated to accomplish these arts because of their desire to improve their image in the eyes of others, such improvements were not luxurious because God created men in such a way as to use their pride to make them useful to others. "Man," Campbell said, "animated with desire to approve himself to the goodliking and esteem of his own species, will do what he can, to invent, or improve art, science, manufacture, trade; in short whatever can be usefully applied to benefit and comfort mankind" (p. 162). Where was the sin, Campbell asked, in wearing fine clothes for ornament which made our appearances more agreeable to others or in the construction of fine buildings?

Campbell, it would seem, had escaped Mandeville's dilemma simply by denying that pride, vanity, and self-love were vicious and, in the place of the rigorist ethics common in the period and used by Mandeville, substituted the criterion of public benefit, whatever the motive, for virtue. Whereas pride was useful, but outside the realm of virtue, according to Mandeville, in Campbell it was brought within the area of moral acts because it contributed to the public good. Clearly the incorporation of self-love into virtue went a long way toward undermining the distinction found in Mandeville between virtue and commerce, and it was this response that became popular among the Scottish School of philosophers.

However, no matter how far Campbell seemed to go in collapsing the distinction between virtue and commerce, he was unable completely to do away with the idea of luxury, and therefore maintained, albeit in an attenuated form, the tension between virtue and commerce. Campbell believed that the same principles of self-love that justified some actions could also be used to condemn others as luxurious. "So that . . . the pursuit of every pleasure that carries us beyond the self-love or interest of those beings to which we are associated, or that inspires us with any affection, or determines us to any action that is contrary to their good or happiness is luxury" (p. 122). In general luxury was in this case identified with a desire for money or beautiful objects so overwhelming that it caused a man to forget his own welfare, thus contradicting his self-love, and to ruin the welfare of others. His example of this behavior included a man squeezing money from widows or orphans and, perhaps more likely, a man squandering his money so that he ruined the fortunes of himself and his family. This was, in part, the same definition of luxury found in Bluett – living above one's means. Consistent with this view of luxury was the idea that spending appropriate to one class was inappropriate to another. Campbell wrote that "that which is called superfluous, vicious, or luxurious to some degree of people, may be thought requisite to, or be innocently pursued and enjoyed by those of high quality" (p. 125).

The second part of Campbell's view of luxury was based on the distinction between a proper and an improper concern for wealth. So long as an interest in wealth was consistent with the fulfillment of duties to oneself and others it was legitimate. But if this interest became excessive it was called avarice and in a private citizen could lead to the betrayal of one's country. In magistrates avarice was even more catastrophic because it could destroy the administration of government. "Vice and luxury," Campbell concluded, "are irregular passions, that have no bounds, whether in governors or subjects, since they sap the very foundation of society, or confound and overthrow liberty and property, and all good government and even ruin trade itself" (p. 149).

Of all those who felt compelled to write against Mandeville, none was more thorough in his criticism or more important to the history of social thought than Francis Hutcheson. In the years following the publication of *Fable*, vol. 2, during which British moral philosophy flourished, Hutcheson led the way.[17] His works written in this period include two letters in 1724 to the *London Journal* attacking Mandeville, three letters in 1726 to the *Dublin Journal*, which were later collected with three others written against Hobbes and published in 1750 in a volume called *Reflections upon Laughter and Remarks upon the Fable of the Bees, An Inquiry Concerning the Original of our Ideas of Virtue or Moral Good* (1725), *An Essay on the Nature and Conduct of the Passions and Affections and Illustrations on the Moral Sense* (1728), *A System of Moral Philosophy* (written in 1735–37 but not published until 1755), and *A Short Introduction to Moral Philosophy* (1742 Latin, 1747 English). While his targets included Hobbes, La Rochefoucauld, and the rationalist Gilbert Burnet, it is not unfair to say that the main impetus for the development of his thought came from his disagreement with Mandeville. In these works Hutcheson developed the earliest systematic theory of utilitarianism largely to extricate social and moral thought from the Mandevillian paradox of private vices, public virtues. His work was also important because of his identification with the civic humanist tradition, and it may be that he altered the nature of that tradition by reconciling its notions of republican virtue to the demands of the commercial world.

It is not difficult to find in Hutcheson many of those ideas we have come to associate with civic humanism and with the philosophy of public-spiritedness that we recognize as antagonistic to Mandeville's thought. A solitary, solipsistic existence was not natural to man, he began; instead, "the state of nature is that of peace and good will, of innocence and beneficence, and not of violence, war and rapine."[18] Men entered civil society not from force or because of wickedness but, rather, from the mere imperfections of men who were otherwise just and good. In civil society it was the purpose of the magistrates "to promote, by all just and effectual methods, true principles of virtue, such as lead men to piety to God, and all just, peaceable, and kind dispositions toward their fellows . . . ."[19] Education, discipline, and the example of those in power were all needed to promote virtue – both private and public. Instilling virtue in the citizens was so important that every state should have a "censorial power" that "the manners of the people may be regulated, and that luxury, voluptuous debauchery, and other private vices prevented or made infamous, which otherwise would destroy all public virtue, and all faithful regard to the general good, and lead men to ruin the best contrived polity."[20]

Following Harrington, Hutcheson argued that government can be stable only if it "has large property for its foundation."[21] He also favored a mixed government, a two-house legislature with one house popularly elected, and the rotation of magistrates. Even more indicative of his adherence to the principles of civic humanism was his justification for an agrarian law in those situations where the wealth of a few might threaten freedom. Thus, he stated that

> we are never to put in the balance with the liberty or safety of a people, the gratifying the vain ambition, luxury, or avarice of a few. It may therefore often be just to prevent by agrarian law such vast wealth coming into a few hands, that a cabal of them might endanger the state.[22]

Perhaps most important for the political development of that tradition was his contract theory and his justification of resistance. His resistance theories can be found as early as his *Inquiry into the Origin of Moral Virtues* (1726), where he argued that under some circumstances civil war was less odious than bad governments.[23] His popularity in America may be explained by his arguments that justified the rebellion of colonies.[24]

Recently, a scholar has provocatively summarized the civic humanist attitude toward the economic world as "in praise of poverty."[25] Though Hutcheson's political ideas were consistent with this tradition, his economic ideas, despite the hypothetical justification for an agrarian law, were not. Hutcheson, like Mandeville, viewed society through the idea that two alternative kinds of social organization existed. Hutcheson's awareness of a noncommercial society recommended because of its virtue can be found in a section in his *System of Moral Philosophy* in which he provided a justification for income from interest and argued that interest in his society ought to find its own level and not be set artificially by laws regulating its rate. However, he said, there was another kind of society in which interest might not be justified.

> If the polity of any state allows little commerce with foreigners, admits of no great wealth in the hands of a few, nor of any alienation of lands to perpetuity; if it is designed for a republic of farmers, which some great authors judge most adapted for virtue and happiness, then all interest of money might be properly prohibited. But when the strength of a state depends upon trade, such a law would be ruinous.[26]

Hutcheson understood that his own society operated on a set of principles far different from those in a "society of farmers," and took as his task to show against Mandeville, who allowed virtue only in a noncommercial society, that virtue and commerce were compatible. To do this, Hutcheson had to show that the prosperity or luxury of some, which resulted from commerce, was not a threat to virtue, and that men were not motivated to create that prosperity by their narrowly selfish desires.

In one of Hutcheson's first published responses to Mandeville, the three letters to the *Dublin Journal*, he set out to prove that "the consumption of manufactures does not necessarily tend to vice."[27] The discussion focused on the problem of luxury, and Hutcheson advanced a solution that we recognize as a common response to Mandeville. As befitted a moralist, he began by arguing that the truest pleasures consisted in kind affections to other men and that acknowledging this truth would enable a man to be satisfied with the "plainest nourishing food" and with a plain but comfortable house and clothes. Yet, more sumptuous accommodations were not inconsistent with a virtuous life so long as they were consistent with one's station in life. Thus luxury as a vice was not thought of as simply sumptuous living, but was vicious only if the high style was above one's means. "There is," he said, "no sort of food, architecture, dress, or furniture, the use of which can be called an evil in itself." The evil was "using more curious and expensive habitation, dress, table, equipage, than the person's wealth will bear, so as to discharge his duty to his family, his friends, his country, or the indigent" (p. 56).

Hutcheson's view that luxury was relative to social station was not at all new; we have already found it in Bluett, Berkeley, and Campbell. More interesting in these letters, because of the temptation to see Mandeville's rigorism as simply a ploy, is Hutcheson's acceptance of that stance as serious and sincere. He remarked that Mandeville "has probably been struck with some old fanatic sermon upon self-denial in his youth, and can never get it out of his head since" (p. 56).

In Hutcheson's later works we not only find the justification of luxury through the argument that it is relative and not vicious in itself, but we also find passages which, when collected, constitute a rhapsody to the high life. In the *Inquiry* Hutcheson seemed to say that a grand manner of living in persons able to afford such lifestyles was actually a sign of a benevolent nature. The high life carried with it "some appearance of friendship, of love, of communicating pleasures to others, which preserve the pleasures of the luxurious from being nervous and insipid."[28] More specifically, in high living "there is such a mixture of moral ideas, of benevolence, of abilities kindly employed; so many dependents supported, so many friends entertained, assisted, protected; such a capacity imagined for great and amicable action, that we are never ashamed, but rather boast of such things." Hutcheson observed a connection in the minds of most men, against which he did not argue, "between external grandeur, regularity in dress, equipage, retinue, badges of honor, and some moral abilities greater than ordinary." In the same way that men associated wealth with a moral capacity, validly it seems, they believed that "meanness of dress, table, equipage . . . argues . . . avarice, meanness of spirit, want of capacity or conduct in life or industry or moral ability of one kind or another" (p. 139). Whereas Mandeville might have reduced sumptuous eating habits to gluttony, we find that in the *System* Hutcheson stated that "the very luxury of the table derives its main charms from some mixture of moral enjoyments, from communicating pleasures, and notions of something honorable as well as elegant."[29] And in the *Short Introduction* Hutcheson found the origin of luxury not, as Mandeville would, in the prideful nature of man, but instead in the kindness of God. "There is a certain measure of sensual pleasures and elegance both graceful and innocent; to provide us to this degree God and nature have produced many fruits and other materials with exquisite art."[30]

Once Hutcheson had shown that the sumptuousness of the wealthy was not vicious, he had to show that a society made up of virtuous men, content to live within their station, was consistent with the motivations demanded by a trading, commercial nation. Hutcheson had to argue against the notion that mankind was moved to undergo the toils of labour only from avarice and that society flourished only by serving the extravagant, imagined needs of discontented men. It is not surprising then to find that in the *Reflections upon Laughter . . .*, he described men as laboring because they found in work more pleasure than they found in sloth. The discovery of new devices not only increased the happiness of mankind but was enjoyable in itself. As for the problem of maintaining a high level of demand in society (we have already seen that there is no

vice, and much virtue, in the liberal spending of the wealthy)
Hutcheson argued, along with Bishop Berkeley, for one, that a prodigal
would consume more only in the short run, that because of his habits he
was bound to die or become destitute at a young age, and would in the
long run consume less than a man who remained contented with his
position in life and did not spend beyond it. Thus "a sober, frugal
economist, in a long and healthy copious life, generally makes greater
consumption than a prodigal of equal fortune."[31]  While there was vice
in wealthy commercial societies, it was wrong, Hutcheson concluded,
to imagine that the wealth came from the vice. Industry and trade
created wealth and the happiness of citizens. Hutcheson understood
that if one continued, as Mandeville did, to think that trade depended
on viciousness, the debate turned on the definition of vice.

In order to escape the paradox "private vice, public virtue,"
Hutcheson was pushed to develop the utilitarian definition of virtue
that "that action is best, which preserves the greatest happiness for the
greatest numbers."[32]  He extricated himself from Mandeville's dilemma
by arguing that if an action was a public benefit it could not have come
from a private vice. Certainly this summary of Hutcheson's position is
somewhat of an exaggeration because, like any moralist, Hutcheson
had to be concerned with the interior act, and he realized that un-
intended good consequences did not make acts that were motivated by
base motives virtuous, such as a desire to harm someone else. Thus
Hutcheson distinguished between actions materially good that
regardless of motive, benefited the public and acts formally good that
were public benefits resulting from virtuous motives.[33]  And though
Hutcheson stated that magistrates who could not see intention had to
reward actions that tended to the public good regardless of possible
motive, he specifically argued that "no good effect which I do not actually foresee and intend, makes my action morally good."[34]

While Hutcheson believed that there were vicious forms of self-love,
the overall thrust of his work was to narrow the scope of these forms
and to legitimize many other manifestations of self-love. In the same
way that he argued that sumptuousness was not an evil in itself, he
tried to show that self-love was not always vicious. Just as Hutcheson
found the origins of much elegance and exquisite art in God, he also
found that "God has for the benefit of each individual, and of families,
implanted in each one his private appetite and desires, with some
tender affections; in these narrower systems [men and families] actions
flowing from them [private appetites and desires] are naturally approved, or at least deemed innocent. . . ."[35] Hutcheson defined actions
motivated from self-love as vicious only when they took the form of in-
juring someone else. Actions flowing solely from self-love and having no
good or ill effect on others were morally innocent. Thus, he said "actions which flow solely from self-love, and yet evidence no want of

benevolence, having no hurtful effect upon others, seem perfectly in-
different in a moral sense."[36] In fact, insofar as such actions increased
the pleasure of the actor and harmed no one else, they increased the
happiness of the whole and were morally praiseworthy.[37] Implanted by
God, self-love was as important to the proper operation of society as
was benevolence. "Self-love is really as necessary to the good of the
whole, as benevolence; as that attraction which causes the cohesion of
the parts, is as necessary to the regular state of the whole, as
gravitation."[38] Because self-love was necessary and tended to the
public good it was approved by the moral sense.

The importance of this legitimation of self-interest in economic affairs is clear. It enabled Hutcheson to justify individual economic
aggrandizement. He held that "everyone is conceived to have a right to
act or claim whatever does no hurt to others, and naturally tends to his
own advantage. . . ."[39] Because "general benevolence alone, is not a
motive strong enough to industry"[40] and self-love was necessary to
motivate men to "labour and toil," it is morally vicious to deprive men
of their property for it "takes away all motives to industry from
self-love."[41]

This example not only provides us with an insight into the way in
which self-love was justified by Hutcheson, using utility, but it also illustrates Hutcheson's attempt to show that self-love was often mixed
with finer emotions. For Hutcheson the motivation to industry was also
provided by "the strongest attraction of friendship, of gratitude, and
the additional motive of honour."[42] In the *System* we find the same
attitude when Hutcheson stated that men were excited to patience,
diligence, and industry not only by "the hopes of future wealth, ease
and pleasure to themselves . . . [but also to] their offspring, and all
those dear to them, and of some honour to themselves on account of
their ingenuity."[43]

The more refined view of self-love in Hutcheson was also extended to
cover honor and compassion, neither of which Mandeville accepted as
virtuous. While Mandeville took pains to show that honor was based on
self-love and therefore morally reprehensible, Hutcheson, in conscious
disagreement with Mandeville, argued that men honored actions dis-
interestedly from the operation of their moral sense. "Honour,"
Hutcheson averred, "presupposes a sense of something amicable beside
advantage, viz, a sense of excellence in a public spirit; and therefore the
first sense of moral good must be antecedent to honor, for honor is based on it."[44] In the same way, Hutcheson countered Mandeville's belief
that compassion or pity merely self-interested. That our pity was
disinterested and had for its object the distress of the person we observed was proved, according to Hutcheson, because we were moved to aid
the person in distress and not just run away.

While we have found in Bernard Mandeville an apology for commercial society, it was an apology, as I have emphasized throughout, based solely on the material benefits of such a society – morally, commercial society in Mandeville's work was condemned. Mandeville was able to carry off this paradoxical apology because of his acceptance of a rigorist morality, which demanded that self-interest be transcended, and because of his psychological investigations, which uncovered self-interest everywhere. Though we have seen that many after Mandeville sought to reconcile commerce and moral principles, it fell to Francis Hutcheson to provide a systematic defense of commercial society in such a way as to make the principles of that society consistent with the principles of virtue. Furthermore, this task was carried out within the tradition of civic humanism. The system he created accomplished this reconciliation by changing the standard of morality to utility and by using the idea of a moral sense to emphasize the importance of benevolence in human nature. He reinterpreted sumptuousness to show its moral qualities, argued that men labored for the benefit of others as well as themselves, and made morally legitimate many forms of self-love. It was only fitting that Hutcheson should have relied so heavily in his disagreement with Mandeville on the Stoic tradition – Cicero, Pufendorf, Grotius, and Shaftesbury – which the Jansenists, who provided so much to Mandeville, sought to destroy.

The distinction Mandeville drew between the material benefits of a commercial society and the moral ill effects occasioned by that type of society provided the impetus for much of the debate that raged in the first half of the eighteenth century over luxury and trade. It may be that his work met with such outrage because there was a general and widespread uneasiness about a society dominated by trade. As we have seen, even those who went far toward accepting luxury and self-interest reaffirmed the values of simplicity and stressed the importance of public-spiritedness to the cohesion of society. If in the consideration of Mandeville's critics we have found a more and more lenient attitude toward the principles of the commercial world, there is no better way to conclude than to survey briefly two of the essays of David Hume. In "Of Commerce" and "Of Refinement in the Arts" we find finally the belief that commercial society and the spread of luxury actually contribute to progress in morals. The importance of Mandeville to these essays not only is apparent from their general structure and arguments, but can be seen clearly by the footnote reference in "Of Commerce" to J. F. Melon,[45] perhaps the only clear follower of Mandeville, and in "Of Refinement in the Arts" to Mandeville himself.

Hume set out to show that "the greatness of a state and . . . the happiness of its subjects . . . are . . . inseparable with regard to commerce."[46] To accomplish this reconciliation he first reproduced the argument, with considerable more clarity than could be found among its supporters, which tied the wealth and power of the state to the poverty of its citizens. If, the argument went, the wants and needs of men were few, it would take but a part of the kingdom to supply those wants. The superfluous hands would then be able to staff the army and the fleet to make the nation strong. Luxury was dangerous because it would increase the wants of men, which would decrease the number of men available for military service. Nor, said Hume, was this thinking fanciful, for it was based on the history of Rome and Sparta.

Yet, however well these principles worked for earlier societies, it was not, according to Hume, possible to return to them because of the changed historical circumstances. These states were free, small, with equality of fortune, and all existed in the martial age of continual public alarm. These were not the conditions in which most states found themselves in the eighteenth century. And rather than emulate the early republics, "Sovereigns must take mankind as they find them, and cannot pretend to introduce any violent change in their principles and ways of thinking." In the natural course of affairs, Hume said, "that policy is violent which aggrandizes the public by the poverty of individuals" (p. 266).

Hume's historical consciousness, his awareness of the importance of the "time and experience" (p. 262) that separated the early frugal, martial republics from his own day, can be seen as part of the legacy of Mandeville's emphasis upon those same topics in his argument with Shaftesbury. But even more important, the central distinction found in Mandeville between a society based on public-spiritedness and a society based on commerce occupied the center of Hume's thought in the essay "Of Commerce." Thus he stated:

> Could we convert a city into a kind of fortified camp, and infuse into each breast so martial a genius, and such a passion for public good, as to make everyone willing to undergo the greatest hardships for the sake of the public, these affections might now, as in ancient times, prove alone a sufficient spur to industry, and support the community. It would then be advantageous, as in camps, to banish all arts and luxury . . . . But as these principles are too disinterested and too difficult to support, it is requisite to govern men by other passions, and animate them with a spirit of avarice and industry, art, and luxury [pp. 268–269].

The spread of the commercial spirit made it impossible to motivate men by using arguments based on public good. Instead society had to rely on harnessing the private desires of men.

However, Hume argued that relying on private passions did not mean the impoverishment of the public or its weakening. In fact, just the opposite occurred. The spread throughout all society of the desire for profit and luxury, the awakening of avarice in all men, motivated men to industry in a way that exhortations of the public, or even compulsions, could never accomplish.

> ... the pleasures of luxury and the profit of commerce; and their delicacy and industry being once awakened, carry them on to further improvements in every branch of domestic as well as foreign trade.... It rouses men from their indolence ... [p. 270].

Because of improvements, fewer men were needed to farm the land and provide the necessities for society and many were set free to work in manufacturers and trade. When war came it was possible to convert many in the manufacturing class to soldiers, to maintain them by the surplus food of farmers and by the taxes on newly created wealth. "The more labour," Hume stated, "that is employed beyond mere necessaries the more powerful is any state; since the persons engaged in that labour may easily be converted to the public service" (p. 268).

Hume had by this argument accomplished two important tasks. First, he had reconciled luxury to the strength and power of the state against those who thought it ennervated men. Second, he had moved beyond the idea that avarice and emulation moved only the wealthy, who in their spending for luxury goods employed the poor, a class moved only by the fear of starvation. Hume envisioned a society where all were made industrious through their private desires for a higher standard of living. In this regard he justified a high level of both exports and imports and did not fear general prosperity and high wages even among the lower orders. "Where ... a number of the labouring poor, as the peasants and farmers, are in very low circumstances, all the rest must partake of their poverty, whether the government of that nation be monarchical or republican" (p. 273).

Having shown in "Of Commerce" that commerce, luxury, and avarice were consistent with a powerful nation, Hume set out in "Of Refinement in the Arts" to show that such a society was also consistent with virtuousness. He began by noting the ambiguity in the word "luxury," stated that "In general I mean great refinement in the gratification of the senses . . .,"[47] and argued that no act of gratification by itself constituted a vice. "Indulgences," he said, "are only vices, when they are pursued at the expense of some virtue" (p. 275), such as caring for family or friends. Nor did he believe that aggregate demand in society depended upon the immoderate gratification of the senses. He advanced the argument that more people benefited if money was invested than if it was spent foolishly.

But, most important, Hume wanted to argue that commercial societies based on the widespread pursuit of luxury, that is to say "ages of refinement, are both the happiest and the most virtuous" (p. 276). The constant preoccupation of men in commerce to find new and better ways to produce or trade had the effect of enlarging the faculties and powers of the mind. A society that constantly advances in "industry and . . . mechanical arts . . . commonly produces some refinement in liberal arts" (p. 276). "The spirit of the age," Hume believed, "affects all the arts, and the minds of men being once roused from their lethargy, and put into fermentation, turn themselves on all sides, and carry improvements into every art and science." The improved methods of farming and industry push men into the cities where they come into contact with many people and "receive and communicate knowledge" (p. 278). As the arts advance, men become more sociable.

They must feel an increase of humanity, from the very habit of con-
vening together, and contributing to each others pleasures and
entertainment. Thus, industry, knowledge and humanity are linked
together, by an indissoluble chain, and are found, from experience
as well as reason, to be peculiar to the more polished, and, what are
commonly denominated, the more luxurious ages [p. 278].

The forces leading to the increased feelings of humanity in men in ages of luxury also had their effects on the operation and institutions of government. New knowledge enabled government to operate more efficiently and to bring to society more order. The increase in the social passions moderated the severity of government actions, which in the past had led to rebellion, and also moderated the actions of those fac-tions that in more primitive times might have embarked upon revolu-tion. In this era in which "factions were less inveterate, revolutions less tragical, authority less severe, and seditions less frequent" (pp. 280–281), it was possible for citizens to exercise more liberty. But, most important for the growth of liberty, societies based on commerce became dominated by "that middling rank of men, who are the best and finest basis of public liberty" (p. 284).

Thus we find in these two essays by Hume the belief that ages of lux-ury were not only more conducive to state power and widespread vir-tuousness, but were also more conducive to liberty. Here is the culmination of the argument over the way to reconcile the traditional categories of social analysis – liberty and virtue – with the demands of a commercial society based on self-interest. This was the argument that occupied early eighteenth-century England and in which Mandeville played so central a role.

# Conclusion

We have found in the work of Bernard Mandeville an analysis and defense of the commercial society that emerged in England following the Restoration of 1660. The social thought of this period was dominated by the categories of virtue and corruption and Mandeville, more than any of his contemporaries, sought to understand and justify the forces that others saw only as corrupting. Because the tradition of civic humanism, recently given considerable attention by scholars, was so central to those who argued that England needed a moral revival, Mandeville's work constitutes one of the most important criticisms of that tradition.

Mandeville's thought was first developed in opposition to a broad movement directed by the Societies for the Reformation of Manners, which were first organized to enforce more strongly the laws against moral offenses. Mandeville continued to oppose the reform movement when its energies shifted to the setting up of Charity Schools for the education of the children of the poor. And in the 1720s, when the enthusiasm behind the reform movement waned, Mandeville continued to develop his thought against the ideas of the third Earl of Shaftesbury. The ideas of both the reformers and Shaftesbury, Mandeville believed, were incompatible with a prosperous and powerful England.

To debunk the arguments for public-spiritedness, Mandeville relied upon two different but interrelated sets of ideas. In both late seventeenth century French moral thought and mercantilism he found a strong emphasis on the importance of self-interest. La Rochefoucauld and La Fontaine, both influenced by Jansenism, provided him with a method of psychological investigation that uncovered the operation of self-love in all human actions. The skeptic Pierre Bayle not only stressed the importance of egoism, but also provided Mandeville with an empiricist theory of knowledge, moral relativism, and a justification for luxury. And from mercantilism he received not only specific doctrines about the poor, the balance of trade, and luxury, but, more basically, a model of society based on the spending of the wealthy and the labor of the poor, all held together by the power of the state.

Mandeville did not just attack rigorist Christian ethics, which when applied to society demanded public-spiritedness. He also provided an analysis of commercial society, which moved beyond the moral interpretation of social life and toward an understanding of how such a society operated and its effects on the nature of man. He understood that a society dominated by commerce brought out the egoism innate in all men. More important, he saw that commercial society was inevitably an urban society and that in an urban setting, where men saw at first hand the styles in which others lived and felt satisfaction in outshining others or pain at not having what others had, vanity was given free rein. In cities men are not bound by the past, they can imagine living in a high style, and because they are well known by so few, they can try to appear to be what they are not. The conspicuous consumption created by commerce and urbanization was seen by Mandeville, as it was by Rousseau, to create vain and avaricious men.

It was the charge of the public-spirited that a society composed of such egoistic men could not cohere. Believing that society held together only through the active promotion of the public good, they feared commercial society because it increased the sense of the private and decreased the awareness of the public. In trying to understand how self-interested men lived together, Mandeville made his most important contributions. By bringing together the ideas of self-interest, empiricism, the division of labor, and the long history of mankind's development, Mandeville was able to explain the operation and material progress of commercial society. And by applying many of these ideas to the state, Mandeville explained how direction could be provided to such a society.

While the enumeration of the principles that brought order and prosperity to commercial societies constituted the most powerful defense of that society, there are in Mandeville other, more obvious, defenses of commercial society. The persistent argument that egoism is innate demonstrated the psychological impossibility of men acting for the public good or constructing a society in which virtue was widespread. Associated with this argument were Mandeville's apology for merchants like Laborio in the *Female Tatler* who are unapologetically self-interested and the attack throughout his writings on aristocrats whose pretensions to honor he traced to pride and self-liking. The argument that it was impossible to give meaning to the idea of luxury, for example, also clearly constituted a defense of commercial society.

However, in order to grasp Mandeville's unique position in the history of social thought it is as important to understand the justification he does not give for commercial society as well as those justifications he does provide. Mandeville never put forward a moral justification for commercial society. Because his defense was carried out in an age that still believed in the duty of men to consider and act upon the public good, he was not able to show the moral praiseworthiness of self-interest. Perhaps it is because his apology was not complete that it illustrates so clearly some of the problems of commercial society. In Mandeville's work we can see that defenders of commercial society must reconcile the demands that men act on self-interest in economics, that they act according to the public interest in their roles as citizens, and that they behave in accordance with the even more universal claims of virtue as moral beings. Such defenders must face the problem that as commercial society sets self-interest, public interest, and virtue against each other, it sets man against himself and his fellows. While Mandeville raises and deals with these problems of commercial society, his purpose was to defend such a society primarily on the grounds that it brought material prosperity and that any more moral alternative was impossible. The incorporation of self-love, and with it commercial society, into the moral world through utilitarianism had to await Hutcheson, Hume, and Smith, who could build, indeed were forced to build, on what Mandeville had written.

# Notes

INTRODUCTION

1. The most complete history and bibliography of this tradition can be found in J. G. A. Pocock, *The Machiavellian Moment*. Also see J. G. A. Pocock, "Civic Humanism and Its Role in Anglo-American Thought," *Politics, Language, and Time*; J. G. A. Pocock, "Virtue and Commerce in the Eighteenth Century," *Journal of Interdisciplinary History*, vol. 3, no. 1, (February 1972): 119–134; Zera S. Fink, *The Classical Republicans* (Evanston, Ill.: Northwestern University Press, 1945); Caroline Robbins, *The Eighteenth-Century Commonwealthman*.

2. See Isaac F. Kramnick, *Bolingbroke and His Circle: The Politics of Nostalgia in the Age of Walpole*; and P. G. M. Dickson, *The Financial Revolution in England*. A short analysis of the economic changes in this period can be found in chapter 4, "Mandeville and Mercantilism".

3. John Trenchard and Thomas Gordon, *Cato's Letters*, February 28, 1720, no. 18.

4. The best discussion of this "country ideology" can be found in Kramnick, *Bolingbroke and His Circle*; also see J. G. A. Pocock, "Machiavelli, Harrington and English Political Ideologies in the Eighteenth Century," *Politics, Language, and Time*.

5. Bernard Mandeville, *Free Thoughts on Religion, the Church, and National Happiness*, p. 355.

6. *Ibid.*, p. 254.

7. See also Richard I. Cook, *Bernard Mandeville*, chap. 1.

8. Benjamin Franklin, *Autobiography and Other Writings* (New York: New American Library), p. 57.


CHAPTER 1. MANDEVILLE AND THE REFORMATION OF MANNERS

1. Edward Stephens, *The Beginning and Progress of a . . . Reformation . . .* (1691), p. 1.

2. *Ibid.*, p. 4.

3. *A Representation of the Societies for the Reformation of Manners* (1715), p. 6.

4. Stephens, *The Beginning and Progress of a . . . Reformation . . .* preface, "To the King."

5. Josiah Woodward, *A Help to a National Reformation . . .* (1706), p. 81.

6. John Disney, *A View of Ancient Laws . . .* (1729), preface.

7. Woodward, *A Help to a National Reformation. . . .*

8. Garnet V. Portus, *Caritas Anglicana*, p. 10.

9. Woodward, *A Help to a National Reformation* . . ., p. 22.

10. Bahlman, *The Moral Revolution of 1688*, chap. 1.

11. Woodward, *A Help to a National Reformation* . . . p. 90.

12. William Bisset, *More Plain English* (1704), p. 6.

13. Isaac Watts, "To Encourage the Reformation of Manners," *Works*, 2: 166.

14. Bahlman, *The Moral Revolution of 1688*, p. 67.

15. James Whiston, *England's State-Distempers* (1704).

16. Bahlman, *The Moral Revolution of 1688*, p. 15.

17. Watts, "To Encourage the Reformation of Manners," p. 148.

18. See W. K. Lowther Clarke, *A History of the S.P.C.K.* and *Eighteenth Century Piety*; Mary G. Jones, *The Charity School Movement*.

19. Bahlman, *The Moral Revolution of 1688*, chap. 3.

20. Sacheverell, *Character of Low Churchmen* (1702) and *Communication of Sin* (1709).

21. See M. Dorothy George, *London Life in the Eighteenth Century* (New York: Capricorn Book, 1965).

22. Bahlman, *The Moral Revolution of 1688*.

23. *A Representation of the Societies*. . . ., p. 3.

24. Watts, "To Encourage the Reformation of Manners," p. 154.

25. *Spectator*, No. 8, March 9, 1711.

26. M. Dorothy George, *London Life in the Eighteenth Century*, p. 318.

27. Woodward, *A Help to a National Reformation*. . . ., p. 4.

28. Whiston, *England's State-Distempers*, p. 3.

29. *Ibid.*, p. 4.

30. *Ibid.*, p. 6.

31. Disney, *A View of Ancient Laws*, introduction.

32. Whiston, *England's State-Distempers*, p. 13.

33. *Ibid.*, p. 8.

34. Watts, "To Encourage the Reformation of Manners," p. 145.

35. Bisset, *More Plain English*, p. 4.

36. Richard Willis, *Sermon Preached before the Societies for the Reformation of Manners* (1704).

37. *Typhon: or the Wars between the Gods and Giants* (1704), pp. 5–6.

38. F. B. Kaye, *The Fable of the Bees*, 1: xxxiii.

39. Mandeville, *Fable of the Bees*, 1: 18.

40. The *Female Tatler* was first attributed to Mandeville by Paul B. Anderson, "Splendor out of Scandal. . . ." *Philological Quarterly*, 15 (1936): 286–300.

41. *Tatler*, Dedication to Mr. Maynwaring, in the collected and reprinted edition, London, 1713.

42. *Tatler*, No. 3, April 16, 1709.

43. *Tatler*, No. 108, December 11, 1709.

44. *Fable*, 1: 39.

45. *Female Tatler*, No. 62, November 25, 1709.

46. *Ibid.*

47. *Ibid.*

48. *Tatler*, No. 96, November 19, 1709.

49. *Female Tatler*, No. 66, December 5, 1709.

50. *Female Tatler*, No. 64, November 30, 1709.

51. *Female Tatler*, No. 80, January 6, 1710.

52. *Female Tatler*, No. 84, January 16, 1710.

53. *Ibid.*

54. *Female Tatler*, No. 109, March 22, 1710.

55. *Female Tatler*, No. 105.

56. *Ibid.*

57. *Tatler*, No. 89, November 3, 1709.

58. *Female Tatler*, No. 109, March 22, 1710.

59. *Fable*, 1: 34.

60. *Ibid.*, p. 52.

61. *Tatler*, No. 87, October 29, 1709.

62. *Fable*, 1: 39–40.

63. See Jones, *The Charity School Movement*.

64. Watts, "An Essay Towards the Encouragement of Charity Schools, *Works*, 9: 4.

65. Jones, *The Charity School Movement*.

66. See Jones, *The Charity School Movement*, pp. 55–71; and Allen & McClure, *Two Hundred Years*.

67. *Guardian*, No. 105, July 11, 1713.

68. *Spectator*, No. 294, February 6, 1712.

69. *Fable*, 1: 253.

70. Jones, *The Charity School Movement*, p. 110.

71. See Trenchard and Gordon, *Cato's Letters*, June 15, 1723, No. 133.

72. See chapter 4, below, for a detailed analysis of the economics involved in Mandeville's criticism of the Charity Schools.

73. *Female Tatler*, No. 93, February 10, 1710.


CHAPTER 2. MANDEVILLE AND THE FRENCH MORAL TRADITION

1. The link between Jansenism and French moral thought in the second half of the seventeenth century is aptly summarized by Anthony Levi: "Not only Pascal and Nicole, but also the most worldly habitués of Mme de Sablé's salon, a la Rochefoucauld and even a Saint-Evremond, wrote against a backdrop of meanings and associations determined in part by the systematic theology of Jansenism." See his *French Moralists* (Oxford: Clarendon Press, 1964), p. 203.

2. See, for example, the essays "Of Vanity" and "The Useful and the Honorable" in Donald Frame, *The Complete Essays of Montaigne* (Stanford, Calif.: Stanford University Press, 1954). In "Of Vanity," Montaigne describes a "workable and regular society" set up by King Phillip, populated by wicked men and held together "by their very vices." And in "The Useful and the Honorable" he argues more generally that "vices find their place . . . and are employed for sewing society together. . . ."

3. See Archibald Campbell, *Enquiry into the Original of Moral Virtue* (1728); George Blewitt, *An Enquiry whether the general practice of virtue tends to wealth or poverty* (1725); William Law, *Remarks upon a Late Book . . .* (1724).

4. *Tatler*, No. 108, December 17, 1709.

5. Nigel Abercrombie, *The Origins of Jansenism* (London: Cambridge University Press, 1936), pp. 87–92.

6. *Ibid.*, p. xi.

7. Paul Benichou, *Man and Ethics*, p. 75.

8. Lucien Goldmann, *The Hidden God.* See chapters 3–4 in Goldmann for a more detailed analysis of the social position of the Jansenists.

9. Benichou, *Man and Ethics.*

10. Blaise Pascal, *Pensées*, ed. A. J. Krailsheimer (Baltimore, Md.: Penguin Books, 1966), p. 33.

11. Jacques Esprit, *The Deceitfulness of Human Virtues* (1708), preface.

12. *Ibid.*

13. *Ibid.*, pp. 37–38.

14. Pierre Nicole, *Essais de Moral* (1713), 2: 145, as quoted in Lionel Rothkrug, *Opposition to Louis XIV* (Princeton, N.J.: Princeton University Press, 1965), p. 51.

15. Nicole, *Traite de la Charité et de l'Amour-propre*, chap. 11; from Marcel Raymond, "Du jansenisme à la morale de l'intérêt," *Mercure de France*, June 1957, pp. 238–255 (translation by T.A.H.).

16. See Arthur Lovejoy, *Reflections on Human Nature*, chap. 5.

17. See Rothkrug, *Opposition to Louis XIV*, on "Jansenist utilitarianism."

18. Goldmann, *The Hidden God*, p. 60.

19. W. G. Moore, *La Rochefoucauld: His Mind and Art*, p. 7.

20. See Moore, *La Rochefoucauld: His Mind and Art*, p. 52.

21. La Rochefoucauld, *Maxims*, ed. Louis Kronenberger (New York: Random House, 1959), No. 10.

22. Bernard Mandeville, *Aesop Dressed* (Los Angeles, Calif.: Augustine Reprint Society, No. 120, 1966), preface.

23. "The Carp" appeared in *Female Tatler*, No. 97; "The Hands and Feet and Belly," No. 100; and "The Wolves and the Sheep," No. 98.

24. Bernard Mandeville, *Free Thoughts on Religion, The Church and National Happiness* (1720), p. xx. E. D. James maintains that he has found seventy allusions to Bayle in Mandeville's work. See "Faith, Sincerity and Morality: Mandeville and Bayle," in Irwin Primer, ed. *Mandeville Studies.*

25. *Censura Temporum* (August 1708), 1: 222, 228.

26. Pierre Bayle, *Philosophic Commentary . . . .* as quoted in Sandberg, ed., *The Great Contest Between Reason and Faith* (New York: Ungar, 1963), p. 55.

27. Pierre Bayle, Dictionary *Historical and Critical* vol. II (London, 1735, Second Edition), p. 202.

28. Pierre Bayle, *Miscellaneous Reflections on the Comet . . .* (1708), 2: 382.

29. *Ibid.*, 1: 269.

30. *Ibid.*, p. 279.

31. *Ibid.*, 2: 347.

32. *Ibid.*

33. See *Ibid.*, 2: 339.

34. *Ibid.*, 1: 291.

35. *Ibid.*, 2: 336.

36. *Ibid.*, p. 333.

37. Bayle, *Continuation des Pensées Diverses*, chap. 124, p. 360 (translation by T. A. H.).

38. *Ibid.*, p. 361 (translation by T.A.H.).

39. Bayle, *Miscellaneous Reflections*, 2: 333.

40. Benichou, *Man and Ethics*, pp. 117–37.

41. Rothkrug, *Opposition to Louis XIV*, pp. 67–68.

CHAPTER 3. MANDEVILLE AND SHAFTESBURY

1. *Fable*, 1: 184–85.

2. *Fable*, 1: 324. For some similarities between Mandeville and Shaftesbury, see Irwin Primer, "Mandeville and Shaftesbury," in *Mandeville Studies*.

3. See Benichou, *Man and Ethics*.

4. Anthony Ashley Cooper, third Earl of Shaftesbury, *Characteristics of Men, Manners, Opinions, Times* (Indianapolis, Ind.: Bobbs-Merrill), 2: 98.

5. *Ibid.*, p. 93.

6. *Ibid.*, 1: 240.

7. *Ibid.*, p. 74.

8. *Ibid.*, p. 286.

9. *Ibid.*

10. *Ibid.*, p. 287.

11. *Ibid.*, p. 282.

12. *Ibid.*, 2: 137.

13. *Ibid.*, 1: 27.

14. *Ibid.*, p. 249.

15. See 1: 321–30; 2: 345.

16. *Ibid.*, 1: 72.

17. Leslie Stephen, *English Thought in the 18th Century*, 2: 34.

18. *Fable*, 1: 323–24. Though Shaftesbury certainly thinks benevolence plays a larger role in the world than Mandeville does, he is not as naïvely optimistic as Mandeville suggests. Shaftesbury's point is not that men do not sometimes act selfishly, or that it is easy to act morally, but that men are happier when they subordinate themselves to the public. See Hector Monro, *The Ambivalence of Bernard Mandeville*, chap. 5.

19. *Characteristics*, 2: 344.

20. *Fable*, 1: 326.

21. *Fable*, 2: 20.

22. Canan notes to Smith, *The Wealth of Nations*, (New York: Modern Library), p. 3.

23. See Kaye, *The Fable of the Bees*, 1: cxxxiv–cxxxv, and 2: 142. Also see F. A. Hayek, "Dr. Bernard Mandeville," *Proceedings of the British Academy*, vol. 52 (1966).

24. For a longer treatment of Mandeville's empiricism and his *Treatise of the Hypocondriack . . .*, see Hector Monro, *The Ambivalence of Bernard Mandeville*, chap. 3.

25. *Fable*, 2: 161–62.

26. Bernard Mandeville, *A Treatise of the Hypocondriack and Hysterick Diseases* (London, 1730, 3d ed.), p. 38.

27. J. J. Rousseau, *A Discourse on the Origin and Foundations of Inequality among Men* (New York: St. Martin's Press), p. 145.

28. *Fable*, 2: 267.

29. Ronald Paulson, *Hogarth: His Life, Art, and Times* (New Haven, Conn.: Yale University Press, 1974), p. 117.

30. *Fable*, 2: 33.

31. *Ibid.*, pp. 31–32.

32. See the introduction by John Shea, *Aesop Dressed . . .* (Los Angeles, Calif.: Augustine Reprint Society, 1970).

33. Paulson, *Hogarth*, p. 158.

34. *Fable*, 2: 12.

35. The view that rules of honor were consistent with the precepts of Christianity can be found in Steele, *The Christian Hero* (1701). This work went through twenty editions in the eighteenth century.

36. *Fable*, 2: 65.

37. For the origins of this distinction, see E. D. James, "Faith, Sincerity and Morality: Mandeville and Bayle," *Mandeville Studies*, pp. 53–54; and Malcolm Jack, "Progress and Corruption in the Eighteenth Century: Mandeville's Private Vices, Public Benefits," *Journal of the History of Ideas* (April–June 1976), 37: 369–76. The distinction Mandeville makes between self-love and self-liking is akin to the distinction Rousseau will draw between *amour de soi* and *amour-propre* in the *Discourse on the Origin of Inequality*. Adam Smith was so struck by this and other similarities in Rousseau and Mandeville that he wrote that "the second volume of *The Fable of the Bees* has given occasion to the system of Mr. Rousseau," in *The Early Writings of Adam Smith*, ed. Lindgren (New York: A. M. Kelly, 1967), p. 24.

38. *Fable*, 2: 133.

39. Bernard Mandeville, *An Enquiry into the Origin of Honour and the Usefulness of Christianity in War* (London, 1732), pp. 6–7.

40. *Fable*, 1: 34.

41. Benichou, *Man and Ethics*, p. 119.

42. *Fable*, 1: 36.

CHAPTER 4. MANDEVILLE AND MERCANTILISM

1. See Eli F. Heckscher, *Mercantilism*, esp. vol. 2, part 5.

2. *Ibid.*, p. 293.

3. See P. G. M. Dickson, *The Financial Revolution in England*, and Isaac Kramnick, *Bolingbroke and His Circle*.

4. Eli F. Heckscher, *Mercantilism*, p. 410.

5. Ralph Davis, *A Commercial Revolution: English Overseas Trade in the Seventeenth and Eighteenth Centuries*.

6. See William Letwin, *The Origins of Scientific Economics: English Economic Thought 1660–1776*.

7. Ralph Davis, *A Commercial Revolution*, p. 4.

8. These figures can be found in either Ralph Davis, *A Commercial Revolution* or Ralph Davis, "English Foreign Trade, 1660–1700," in Carus-Wilson, *Essays in Economic History*, vol. 2 (New York: St. Martin's Press, 1962).

9. *Ibid.*

10. Davis, "English Foreign Trade, 1660–1700," p. 259.

11. K. G. Davies, "Joint Stock Investment in the Late Seventeenth Century," in Carus-Wilson, *Essays in Economic History*, 2: 274.

12. Davis, "English Foreign Trade, 1660–1700," p. 258.

13. Davis, *A Commercial Revolution*, p. 14.

14. P. G. M. Dickson, *The Financial Revolution in England*.

15. K. G. Davies, "Joint Stock Investment in the Late Seventeenth Century," in Carus-Wilson, *Essays in Economic History*, 2: 281.

16. Kramnick, *Bolingbroke and His Circle*, pp. 44–45.

17. P. G. M. Dickson, *The Financial Revolution in England*, p. 41.

18. *Ibid.*, p. 46.

19. A. H. John, "Aspects of English Economic Growth in the First Half of the Eighteenth Century," in Carus-Wilson, *Essays in Economic History*, vol. 2.

20. *Ibid.*, p. 373.

21. See H. J. Habakkuk, "English Landownership 1680–1740," in *Economic History Review*, (1940) 10: 2–17; and H. J. Habakkuk, "England," in A. Goodwin (ed.), *The European Nobility in the Eighteenth Century* (London: Adam and Charles Black, 1953).

22. Habakkuk, "English Landownership 1680–1740."

23. Kramnick, *Bolingbroke and His Circle.*

24. Bolingbroke, *The Idea of a Patriot King* (Indianapolis: Bobbs-Merrill, 1965), p. 6.

25. *Cato's Letters*, February 25, 1720, No. 18.

26. *Ibid.*

27. *Cato's Letters*, July 1, 1721, No. 35.

28. *Ibid.*

29. *Miscellaneous Works of Monsieur de St. Evremond*, (London, 1714), 3: 143.

30. *Ibid.*, pp. 140–41.

31. *Ibid.*, 1: 3

32. *Ibid.*, pp. 43–83.

33. *Ibid.*, p. 145.

34. Pierre Bayle, *Pensées Diverses*, p. 361 (translation by T.A.H.).

35. Heckscher, *Mercantilism*, 2: 290.

36. *Ibid.*, pp. 290–91.

37. Lionel Rothkrug, *Opposition to Louis XIV: The Social and Political Origins of the French Enlightenment*, p. 104.

38. See W. J. Ashley, "The Tory Origins of Free Trade Policy," *Surveys, Historic and Economic* (London: Longmans, Green, 1900), pp. 268–303.

39. *Ibid.*

40. Nicholas Barbon, *A Discourse on Trade* (London, 1690), ed. Jacob Hollander (Baltimore, Md.: Johns Hopkins University Press, 1905), p. 10.

41. Dudley North, *Discourse upon Trade* (London, 1691), p. 27.

42. André Morize, *L'Apologie du Luxe au XVIII<sup>e</sup> siècle et "Le Mondain" de Voltaire; étude critique sur le Mondain et ses sources* (Paris, 1909), p. 69 (translation by T.A.H.).

43. Heckscher, *Mercantilism*, 2: 291.

44. E. A. J. Johnson, *Predecessors of Adam Smith*, p. 295.

45. *Fable*, 1:25.

46. Sir William Temple, *Observations Upon the United Provinces of the Netherlands*, In *Works*, (London, 1814), 1: 175.

47. *Ibid.*, p. 176.

48. *Fable*, 1: 183.

49. *Ibid.*, p. 187.

50. See Elizabeth Rawson, *The Spartan Tradition in European Thought* (London: Oxford University Press, 1969), for a more general discussion of the image of Sparta.

51. *Fable*, vol. 1, p. 245.

52. Heckscher, *Mercantilism*, 1: 22.

53. *Fable*, 1: 185.

54. Jacob Viner, *Studies in the Theory of International Trade*, p. 8.

55. *Fable*, 1: 109.

56. The most straightforward interpretation of Mandeville as a laissez-faire economist can be found in F. B. Kaye's introduction to *The Fable of the Bees*. Jacob Viner categorically denies this interpretation in "Introduction to Bernard Mandeville's A Letter to Dion," *The Long View and the Short* (Glencoe, Ill.: The Free Press, 1953). The most interesting attempt to find some middle position for Mandeville that is neither wholly mercantilist nor wholly laissez-faire is in Nathan Rosenberg, "Mandeville and Laissez-faire," *Journal of the History of Ideas*, Vol. 29 (April-June 1963). For other commentators on Mandeville's economic views see in the bibliography works by Albert Shatz, F. Gregoire, Alfred Chalk, and F. A. Hayek.

To argue as I do that both Mandeville's international and domestic economic ideas can best be understood as mercantilist is not to argue that he holds all of the doctrines found among mercantilists in earlier periods. Mercantilism changed during its history and in the early eighteenth century it exhibited some traits that moved it closer to liberalism. Mandeville's specific version of the balance-of-trade doctrine illustrates this change, as does his argument against the Charity Schools that the market ought to set the number of tradesmen. But, while Mandeville's thought is consistent with the liberal elements in later mercantilism, it remained fundamentally mercantilist. Discussions of the liberal components of mercantilism can be found in the bibliography in works by William D. Grampp, E. A. J. Johnson, Alfred Espinas, and Albert Schatz.

57. *Fable*, 1: 115–16.

58. Heckscher, *Mercantilism*, 1: 25.

59. Edgar S. Furniss, *The Position of the Laborer in a System of Nationalism*, p. 42.

60. *Fable*, 1: 279–80.

61. E. J. Hobsbawm, *Industry and Empire* (Baltimore, Md.: Penguin Books, 1968), pp. 40–41.

62. *Fable*, 1: 287.

63. *Cato's Letters*, June 15, 1723, No. 133.

64. Furniss, *The Position of the Laborer in a System of Nationalism*, pp. 7–8.

65. T. E. Gregory, "The Economics of Employment in England, 1660–1713," *Economica* (1921–22), 1: 45.

66. Adam Smith, *The Wealth of Nations* (New York: Modern Library, 1937), pp. 78–79.

67. See note no. 56 in this chapter.

68. Josiah Child, *A New Discourse on Trade* (1690), p. ix.

69. See John Carey, *A Discourse on Trade* (1691), pp. 97–102 in the 1745 edition; and Dudley North, *Discourse upon Trade* (1691). Also see D. C. Coleman, "Labour in the English Economy of the Seventeenth Century," in Carus-Wilson, *Essays on Economic History*, vol. 3; and T. E. Gregory, "The Economics of Employment in England, 1660–1713."

70. For an example of this view, see Samuel Chandler, *A Sermon Preached for the Benefit of the Charity School in Gravel-Lane, Southwark, January 1727/8. To Which is added An Answer to an Essay on Charity-Schools by the Author of the Fable of the Bees* (London, 1728). Chandler argues that the Charity Schools inspired the children of the poor "with a desire to please, by their faithfulness, diligence and industry . . . so they may discharge the duties of the lower stations of life."

71. Isaac Watts, *An Essay Towards the Encouragement of Charity Schools Particularly Among Protestant Dissenters* in *The Works of Isaac Watts* (Leeds: Edwards Barners, 1813), 6: 9.

72. William Hendley, *A Defense of Charity Schools* (London, 1725), pp. 27–28.

73. George Bluett, *An Enquiry whether a General Practice of Virtue Tends to the Wealth or Poverty, Benefit or Disadvantage of a People* (London, 1725).

74. Albert Schatz, *L'individualisme économique et social* (Paris: Libraire Armand Colin, 1907) and Albert Schatz, "Bernard de Mandeville," in *Vierteljahrschrift für Social-und wirtschaftsgeschichte* (1903) 1: 434–480. According to Schatz one finds in Mandeville "tous les germes essentiels de la philosophie économique et sociale de l'individualisme" (p. 62 in his book). And F. B. Kaye in his introduction to Mandeville's *Fable* argues "that Mandeville's exposition of the individualistic position was incomparably the most brilliant, the most complete, the most provocative, and the best known until Adam Smith's . . . (p. cxl). Against this view, see Jacob Viner, "Introduction to Bernard Mandeville, A Letter to Dion" in *The Long View and the Short*. See also F. A. Hayek, *Individualism and Economic Order* (Chicago, Ill.: University of Chicago Press, 1948); and J. A. W. Gunn, "Mandeville and Wither: Individualism and the Workings of Providence," *Mandeville Studies*.

75. Edgar S. Furniss, *The Position of the Laborer in a System of Nationalism*, p. 87.

76. Jacob Viner, *Studies in International Trade*, p. 93.

77. Francis Hutcheson, *Reflections on Laughter and Remarks upon the Fable of the Bees* (London, 1750).

78. T. E. Gregory, "The Economics of Employment in England, 1660–1713," p. 37. The same point is made by William Letwin, *The Origins of Scientific Economics*, p. 3.

79. *Fable*, 1: 7. Italics added.

80. *Ibid.*, p. 369. Italics added.

81. *Ibid.*, p. 412. Italics Mandeville's. The vindication orginally appeared in the *London Journal*, August 10, 1723.

82. *Letter to Dion* (London, 1732) p. 37. Italics added.

83. *Fable*, 2: 187–88.

84. *Fable*, 1: 3.

85. *Fable*, 2: 330.

86. For a different view, see those authors listed in note no. 56 in this chapter.

87. *Fable*, 2: 321.

88. *Fable*, 1: 115–16.

89. *Fable*, 2: 321.

90. *Ibid.*, p. 335.

91. *Ibid.*, p. 322. While Mandeville must, in general, be considered a court Whig, he did manage to keep some distance between himself and Walpole. Compare this statement of Mandeville's which undervalues the importance of any one man, with one by William Arnall, a Walpole apologist, in the *Free Briton*, no. 3. December 18, 1729: "The assistance of a single genius sometimes effects more than the laborious drudgery of an age; and learning has even owed more to the accidental discoveries of very acute minds, than to the painful endeavours of vigilant dunces." See also, H. T. Dickinson, "The Politics of Bernard Mandeville," *Mandeville Studies*.

92. *Ibid.*, p. 325.

93. Bernard Mandeville, *Free Thoughts on Religion, the Church, and National Happiness* (London, 1720), p. 253. The distinction Mandeville makes in this statement has led some to find in his thought an early form of functionalism. See

Louis Schneider, "Mandeville as Forerunner of Modern Sociology," *Journal of the History of the Behavioral Sciences* 6, No. 3 (July 1970): 219–230; and J. A. W. Gunn, "Mandeville and Wither: Individualism and the Workings of Providence," *Mandeville Studies.*

CHAPTER 5. MANDEVILLE AND HIS CRITICS

1. *Fable.*, 1:51.

2. See Bishop Butler, *Fifteen Sermons Preached at the Rolls Chapel* (London, 1726), esp. sermon XI, "Upon the Love of our Neighbour"; William Law, *Remarks upon a Late Book, Entitled the Fable of the Bees* (London, 1724), section 2; Bishop Berkeley, *Alciphron; or the Minute Philosopher,* in *Complete Works,* vol. 2, ed. A. C. Fraser; Robert Burrow, *A Dissertation on the Happy Influence of Society Merely Civil* (London, 1726), and *Civil Society and Government Vindicated* (London, 1723).

3. Edmund Gibson, Bishop of London, *Pastoral Letter to the People of his diocese.* . . . One of the rare cases in which a contemporary of Mandeville's mentions his work favorably can be found in Matthew Tindal, *An Address to the Inhabitants of London and Westminster* (London, 1729), which was written against Gibson's pastoral letter.

4. Gibson, *Pastoral Letter,* p. 2.

5. Berkeley, *Alciphron* . . ., 2d dialogue; and John Thorold, *A Short Examination of the Notions Advanced in a book entitled the Fable of the Bees* (London, 1726).

6. See Kaye's discussion in *Fable,* 1: xxiii–xxiv.

7. See *An Enquiry into the Causes of the Frequent Executions at Tyburn.*

8. John Thorold, *A Short Examination* . . ., p. 8.

9. John Dennis, *Vice and Luxury Public Mischiefs or Remarks on a Book entitled Fable of the Bees* (London, 1724).

10. George Bluett, *An Enquiry whether the general practice of virtue tends to the wealth or poverty, benefit or disadvantage of a people* (London, 1725).

11. *Ibid.*, preface.

12. Bishop Berkeley, *Alciphron* . . ., pp. 71–74.

13. *Ibid.*, p. 78.

14. In A. C. Fraser, ed. *Complete Works,* 4: 421–76.

15. *Ibid.*, pp. 457–58.

16. Archibald Campbell, *Enquiry into the Original of Moral Virtue* . . . (London, 1728).

17. William Frankena has remarked that "if the writers of the period had been asked to designate who among them was the most original and important they would have picked Hutcheson . . .," in "Hutcheson's Moral Sense Theory," *Journal of the History of Ideas* (1955), pp. 356–75.

18. Francis Hutcheson, *A Short Introduction to Moral Philosophy* (London, 1747), pp. 139–40.

19. Francis Hutcheson, *A System of Moral Philosophy,* vol. 2 (London, 1755), p. 310. Mandeville's use of "politicians" to move men from the state of nature to civil society, perhaps akin to Rousseau's Legislator, can also be seen in Hutcheson, who speaks of "men of superior genius and penetration" convincing the vulgar to "quit their own customs." See *A System of Moral Philosophy,* 2: 214, and *A Short Introduction to Moral Philosophy,* pp. 279, 282.

20. Hutcheson, *A System of Moral Philosophy,* 2: 265.

21. Hutcheson, *A Short Introduction* . . ., p. 295.

22. *Ibid.*, p. 296.

23. Francis Hutcheson, *An Inquiry Concerning the Original of Our Ideas of Virtue or Moral Good*, in L. A. Selby-Bigge ed., *British Moralists* (New York: Dover Publications, 1965). 1: 171. Also see *A Short Introduction* . . ., pp. 303–4, and *A System* . . ., 2: 270.

24. See Caroline Robbins, *The Eighteenth-Century Commonwealthman*, and Bernard Bailyn, *The Ideological Origins of the American Revolution*.

25. J. A. W. Gunn, "Mandeville: Poverty, Luxury and the Whig Theory of Government," paper delivered in Toronto in 1973 at the meeting of the Conference for the Study of Political Thought.

26. Hutcheson, *A System of Moral Philosophy*, 2: 74.

27. Hutcheson, *Reflections upon Laughter and Remarks upon the Fable of the Bees* (London, 1750), p. 56.

28. Hutcheson, *An Inquiry into the Original of our Ideas* . . ., p. 147.

29. Hutcheson, *A System of Moral Philosophy*, p. 86.

30. Hutcheson, *A Short Introduction* . . ., p. 321.

31. *Ibid.*, p. 322.

32. Hutcheson, *An Inquiry into the Original of our Ideas* . . ., p. 107.

33. Hutcheson, *A Short Introduction*, p. 126.

34. Hutcheson, *An Inquiry into the Original of our Ideas*, p. 114.

35. Hutcheson, *A Short Introduction*, p. 120.

36. *Ibid.*, p. 103.

37. *Ibid.*, p. 134.

38. Hutcheson, *An Inquiry into the Original of our Ideas* . . ., p. 164.

39. Hutcheson, *A Short Introduction* . . ., p. 120.

40. Hutcheson, *An Inquiry into the Original of our Ideas* . . ., p. 164.

41. *Ibid.*, p. 165.

42. *Ibid.*, p. 164.

43. Hutcheson, *A System of Moral Philosophy*, 1: 320.

44. Hutcheson, *An Inquiry into the Original of our Ideas* . . ., p. 133. Also see *A System of Moral Philosophy*, vol. 1, chap. 5.

45. J. F. Melon, *Essai Politique sur le Commerce* (1734).

46. David Hume, "Of Commerce," in *Essays, Moral, Political and Literary*.

47. David Hume, "Of Refinement in the Arts," in *Essays Moral, Political and Literary*, p. 275.

# Bibliography

I. SELECTED BIBLIOGRAPHY OF THE WORKS OF BERNARD MANDEVILLE

*Aesop Dressed; or, a Collection of Fables Writ in Familiar Verse.* London, 1704.

*Typhon; or, the Wars between the Gods and Giants: A Burlesque Poem in Imitation of the Comical Mons. Scarron.* London, 1704.

*The Grumbling Hive; or, Knaves Turn'd Honest.* London, 1705.

*The Virgin Unmasked; or, Female Dialogues betwixt an Elderly Maiden Lady and her Niece.* London, 1709.

*The Female Tatler.* London, 1709–10.

*A Treatise on the Hypocondriak and Hysterick Passions.* London, 1711.

*Wishes to a Godson, with Other Miscellany Poems.* London, 1712.

*The Fable of the Bees.* [Vol. 1.] London, 1714.

*Free Thoughts on Religion, the Church, and National Happiness.* London, 1720.

*A Modest Defense of Publick Stews.* London, 1724.

*An Enquiry into the Causes of the Frequent Executions at Tyburn.* London, 1725.

*Letters published in the British Journal for April 24 and May 1, 1725.*

*The Fable of the Bees.* Part II. London, 1729.

*An Enquiry into the Origin of Honour, and the Usefulness of Christianity in War.* London, 1732.

*A Letter to Dion, Occasioned by his Book Call'd Alciphron.* London, 1732.


II. SEVENTEENTH- AND EIGHTEENTH-CENTURY SOURCES

A. *Newspapers and Periodicals*
*The British Journal,* 1725–26.
*Cato's Letters,* 1720–23.
*Censura Temporum,* July–August 1708.
*The Craftsman,* January 1731–April 1732.
*The Guardian,* July 11, 1713.
*Present State of the Republic of Letters,* January 1732, February 1732.

*The Spectator,* February 6, 1712.
*The Tatler,* 1709–11.


B. *Books and Pamphlets.*
*An Account of Several Work-Houses for Employing and Maintaining the Poor.*
London, 1732.
Arbuckle, James. *Collection of Letters and Essays on Several Subjects, lately
published in the Dublin Journal.* Vol. 2. London, 1729.
Barbon, Nicholas. *A Discourse on Trade.* London, 1690.
Bayle, Pierre. *Continuation des Pensées Diverses.* Rotterdam, 1721.
—— *Dictionary, Historical and Critical.* 5 vols. London, 1734–38.
—— *Miscellaneous Reflections Occasioned by the Comet of 1680.* London,
1708.
Bellers, John. *An Essay for Employing the Poor to Profit.* London, 1723.
—— *Proposal for Raising a College of Industry.* London, 1696.
Berkeley, George. *Alciphron; or, the ,Minute Philosopher; containing an
apology for the Christian Religion against those who are Called Free-Thinkers.*
Ed. A. C. Fraser. *Complete Works,* vol. 2. Oxford: Clarendon Press.
1901.
—— *The Querist.* London, 1735–36–37.
Bisset, William. *More Plain English* ... London, 1704.
Bluett, George. *An Enquiry Whether the General Practice of Virtue Tends to the
Wealth or Poverty, the Benefit or Disadvantage of a People.* London, 1725.
Brown, John. *Essays on the Characteristics.* London, 1751.
Burrow, Robert. *A Dissertation on the Happy Influence of Society Merely Civil.*
London, 1726.
—— *Civil Society and Government Vindicated.* London, 1723.
Butler, Joseph. *Fifteen Sermons Preached at Rolls Chapel.* London, 1726.
Campbell, Archibald. *An Enquiry into the Original of Moral Virtue wherein it
is shewn (against the Author of the Fable of the Bees, &c) that Virtue is found-
ed in the Nature of Things* ... London, 1728.
Carey, John. *A Discourse on Trade.* London, 1690.
Chandler, Samuel. *A Sermon Preached for the Benefit of the Charity Schools in
Gravel Lane* ... *To which is added An Answer to an Essay on Charity Schools
by the Author of the Fable of the Bees.* London, 1728.
Child, Josiah. *A New Discourse on Trade.* London, 1690.
Davenant, Charles. *Discourses on the Public Revenues and on Trade.* Ed.
Charles Whitworth. London, 1771.
Defoe, Daniel. *Defense of a Sermon Preached by W. Hendley* ... London,
1719.
—— *Everybodys Business Is Nobodys Business.* London, 1725.
—— *Giving Alms, Not Charity.* London, 1704.
—— *On the Reformation of Manners.* London, 1702.
Dennis, John. *Vice and Luxury Public Mischiefs; or, Remarks on a Book in-
titled, Fable of the Bees.* London, 1724.

Disney, John. *A View of Ancient Laws Against Immortality and Profaneness.* London, 1729.

Esprit, Jacques. *Discourses on the Deceitfulness of Human Virtues.* Trans. William Veauvoir. London, 1706.

Fiddes, Richard. *General Treatise of Morality formed from the Principle of Natural Reason Only, with a Preface in Answers to . . . Fable of the Bees.* London, 1726.

Gay, John. *The Beggar's Opera.* London, 1727.

Gervaise, Isaac. *The System or Theory of the Trade of the World.* London, 1720.

Gibson, Edmund. *Directions Given by Edmund Lord Bishop of London to the Masters and Mistresses of the Charity Schools.* London, 1724.

—— *Pastoral Letter to the People of his Diocese Occasioned by Writings in Favour of Infidelity.* London, fifth edition, 1729.

Hendley, William. *A Defense of the Charity-Schools wherein the Many False, Scandalous and Malicious Objections of Those Advocates for Ignorance and Irreligion, the Author of the Fable of the Bees, and Cato's Letters . . . are fully and distinctly answered.* London, 1725.

Hervey, John. *Some Remarks on the Minute Philospher . . .* London, 1732.

Hume, David. *Essays Moral, Political and Literary.* London: Longmans, Green and Co., 1898.

Hutcheson, Francis. *A Short Introduction to Moral Philosophy.* London, 1742 Latin, 1747 English.

—— *A system of Moral Philosophy.* Glasgow, 1755.

—— *An Enquiry Concerning the Original of our Ideas of Virtue or Moral Good.* London, 1725.

—— *An Essay on the Nature and Conduct of the Passions and Affections and Illustrations on the Moral Sense.* London, 1728.

—— *Reflections upon Laughter and Remarks upon the Fable of the Bees.* London, 1750.

Law, William. *Remarks upon a Late Book, Entitled the Fable of the Bees.* London, 1724.

La Fontaine, Jean de. *Fables.* Trans. Marianne Moore. New York: Viking Press, 1954.

La Rochefoucauld, François, Duc de. *Maxims.* Ed. Louis Kronenberger. New York: Random House, 1959.

Montaigne, Michel de. *The Complete Essays of Montaigne.* Ed. Donald M. Frame. Stanford, Calif.: Stanford University Press, 1948.

North, Dudley. *Discourse upon Trade.* London, 1691.

Pascal, Blaise. *Pensées.* Paris: Gallimard, 1936.

*A Representation of the State of the Societies for the Reformation of Manners.* London, 1715.

Saint-Evremond. *The Miscellaneous Works of Monsieur de St. Evremond.* London, 1714.

Shaftesbury, Anthony Ashley Cooper, third Earl of. *Characteristics of*

*Men, Manners, Opinions, Times.* London, 1711.

Smith, Adam. *The Wealth of Nations.* London, 1776.

Steele, Richard. *The Christian Hero.* London, 1701.

Stephens, Edward. *The Beginning and Progress of a Needful and Hopeful Reformation* . . . London, 1691.

Temple, Sir William. *Observations upon the United Provinces of the Netherlands.* In *Works*, vol. 1. London, 1814.

Thorold, John. *A Short Examination of the Notions Advanc'd in a Late Book intitled The Fable of the Bees.* London, 1726.

Tindal, Matthew. *An Address to the Inhabitants of London and Westminster* . . . London, 1729.

—— *The True Meaning of the Fable of the Bees.* London, 1726.

Watts, Isaac. *To Encourage the Reformation of Manners.* In *Works*, vol. 2. Leeds: Edward Barnes, 1812.

—— *An Essay Towards the Encouragement of Charity Schools.* In *Works*, vol. 6. Leeds: Edward Barnes, 1812.

Whiston, James. *England's State-Distempers, traced from their Originals: with proper remedies and means to make her Virtuous and Prosperous.* London, 1704.

—— "The True Method of Educating Children." In *Sermons*, vol. 3. Bath: Richard Cruttwell, 1822.

Wilson, Thomas. "The Duty of Self-Denial." In *Sermons*, vol. 3. Bath: Richard Cruttwell. 1822.

Woodward, Josiah. *A Help to a National Reformation* . . . London, fifth edition, 1706.


III. MODERN SECONDARY SOURCES


Allen, W. O. B. and Edmund McClure. *Two Hundred Years, 1698–1898: The History of the SPCK.* London: SPCK, 1898.

Anderson, Paul Bunyan. "Cato's Obscure Counterpart in The British Journal 1722–1725," *Studies in Philology* (1937), 34: 412–28.

—— "Innocence and Artifice: Or Mrs. Centilivre and the Female Tatler," *Philological Quarterly* (1937), 16:358–75.

—— "Splendor out of Scandal: The Lucinda-Artesia Papers in the Female Tatler," *Philological Quarterly* (1936), 15:286–300.

Ashley, W. J. "The Tory Origin of Free Trade Policy." In *Surveys Economic and Historic*, pp. 268–303. London: Longmans, Green, 1900.

Ashton, T. S. *An Economic History of England: The Eighteenth Century.* New York: Barnes and Noble, 1955.

Bahlman, Dudley W. P. *The Moral Revolution of 1688.* New York: Archon Books, 1968.

Benichou, Paul. *Man and Ethics.* Garden City, N.Y.: Doubleday, 1971.

Bremond, Henri. *A Literary History of Religious Thought in France*, vol. 1.

translated. London: Society for Promoting Christian Knowledge, 1928.

Broad, C. D. *Five Types of Ethical Theory.* New York: Harcourt, Brace, 1930.

Broad, C. D. "Berkeley's Theory of Morals." *Revue International de Philosophies* (1939), 32: 29–51.

Buck, Philip W. *The Politics of Mercantilism.* New York: Henry Holt, 1942.

Chalk Alfred, "Mandeville's Fable of the Bees: A Reappraisal," *Southern Economic Journal* (1966), 33:1–16.

—— "Natural Law and the Rise of Economic Individualism in England," *Journal of Political Economy* (1951), 59:332–47.

Chiasson, Elias J. "Bernard Mandeville: A Reappraisal," *Philological Quarterly* (1970), 49:489–519.

Clarke, W. K. Lowther. *A History of the S.P.C.K.* London: Society for Promoting Christian Knowledge, 1959.

—— *Eighteenth-Century Piety.* London: Society for Promoting Christian Knowledge, 1944.

Coleman, D. C. "Labour in the English Economy of the Seventeenth Century," In E. M. Carus-Wilson, ed., *Essays in Economic History,* 2:291–309. New York: St. Martin's Press, 1962.

Coleman, D. C., ed. *Revisions in Mercantilism.* London: Methuen, 1969.

Coleman, John. "Bernard Mandeville and the Reality of Virtue," *Philosophy* (1972), 47:125–39.

Cook, Richard I. *Bernard Mandeville.* New York: Twayne, 1974.

Courtines, Leo Pierre. *Bayle's Relations with England and the English.* New York: Columbia University Press, 1938.

Davis, Ralph. *A Commercial Revolution: English Overseas Trade in the Seventeenth and Eighteenth Centuries.* London: Historical Associates, 1967.

—— "English Foreign Trade, 1660–1700." In E. M. Carus-Wilson, ed., *Essays in Economic History,* 2:257–73. New York: St. Martin's Press, 1962.

Dickson, P. G. M. *The Financial Revolution in England.* New York: St. Martin's Press, 1967.

Dobbes, A. E. *Education and Social Movements, 1700–1850.* New York: Augustus M. Kelley, 1969.

Dobree, Bonamy. *English Literature in Early Eighteenth Century, 1700–1740.* Oxford: Clarendon Press, 1959.

—— *Variety of Ways.* Oxford: Clarendon Press, 1932.

Edwards, Thomas. "Mandeville's Moral Prose," *ELH* (1964), 31:195–212.

Espinas, Alfred. "La troisième phase et la dissolution du mercantilisme," *Revue Internationale de Sociologie* (1902), 10:161–80.

Feiling, Keith. *The Second Tory Party, 1714–1832.* Oxford: Clarendon

Press, 1959.

Fisher, F. J. "The Development of London as a Centre of Conspicuous Consumption in the Sixteenth and Seventeenth Centuries." In E. M. Carus-Willson, ed., *Essays in Economic History*, 2:197–208. New York: St. Martin's Press, 1962.

Frankena, William. "Hutcheson's Moral Sense Theory," *Journal of the History of Ideas* (1955), 16:356–75.

Furniss, Edgar S. *The Position of the Laborer in a System of Nationalism*. New York: Sentry Press, 1965.

Fuz, J. K. *Welfare Economics in English Utopias*. The Hague: Martinus Nijhoff, 1952.

Gibson, Daniel Z. "A Critical Edition of the Poems of Bernard Mandeville." Dissertation, University of Cincinnati, 1938.

Golden, Morril. *Fielding's Moral Psychology*. Amherst: University of Massachusetts Press, 1966.

Goldmann, Lucien. *The Hidden God*. New York: Humanities Press, 1964.

Goldsmith, M. M. "Bernard Mandeville." In *International Encyclopedia of Social Science*, vol. 9. New York: Crowell, Collier, Macmillan, 1968.

—— "Introduction." *Enquiry into the Origin of Honor and the Usefulness of Christianity in War*. London: F. Cass, 1971.

—— "Public Virtue and Private Vices: Bernard Mandeville and English Political Ideologies in the Early Eighteenth Century," *Eighteenth-Century Studies* (1976), 9:477–510.

Golgar, B. *The Curse of Party*. Lincoln: University of Nebraska Press, 1961.

Gramp, William D. *Economic Liberalism*. New York: Random House, 1965.

—— "The Liberal Elements in English Mercantilism," *Quarterly Journal of Economics* (1952), 66:465–501.

Green, V. H. H. *The Hanoverians, 1714–1815*. London: Edward Arnold, 1948.

Greene, Donald. "Augustinianism and Empiricism," *Eighteenth-Century Studies* (1967–68), 1:33–69.

Gregory, T. E. "Economics of Employment in England 1660–1713," *Economica* (1921), 1:37–51.

Habakkuk, H. J. "England." In A. Goodwin, ed., *The European Nobility in the Eighteenth Century*. London: Adair and Charles Black, 1953.

—— "English Landownership 1680–1740," *Economic History Review* (1940), 10:2–17.

Harth, Phillip. "Introduction." *Fable of the Bees*. Baltimore: Penguin Books, 1970.

—— "The Satiric Purpose of the Fable of the Bees," *Eighteenth-Century Studies* (1969), 2:321–41.

Hayek, F. A. "Dr. Bernard Mandeville," *Proceedings of The British*

*Academy* (1966), 52:125–41.

Hazard, Paul. *The European Mind, 1680–1715.* New Haven, Conn.: Yale University Press, 1953.

Heckscher, Eli F. *Mercantilism.* 2 vols. London: Allen and Unwin, 1934.

Hughes, P., and Williams, D. (eds.). *The Varied Pattern: Studies in the Eighteenth Century.* Toronto: A. M. Hakkert, 1971.

Hutchinson, T. W. "Berkeley's Querist and Its Place in the Economic Thought of the Eighteenth Century," *British Journal for the Philosophy of Science* (1953), 4:52–78.

Jack, Malcolm. "Progress and Corruption in the Eighteenth Century: Mandeville's Private Vices, Public Benefits," *Journal of the History of Ideas* (1976), 37:369–76.

John, A. H. "Aspects of English Economic Growth in the First Half of the Eighteenth Century." In E. M. Carus-Wilson, ed., *Essays in Economic History*, 2:360–73. New York: St. Martin's Press, 1962.

Johnson, E. A. J. *Predecessors of Adam Smith.* New York: Prentice-Hall, 1937.

Jones, Mary G. *The Charity School Movement: A Study of Eighteenth Century Puritanism in Action.* Cambridge, Eng.: Cambridge University Press, 1938.

Judges, A. V. "The Idea of a Mercantile State," *Transactions of the Royal Historical Society* (1939), 21:41–69.

Kaye, F. B. "The Influence of Bernard Mandeville," *Studies in Philology* (1922), 19:82–108.

—— "The Mandeville Canon," *Notes and Queries* (1924), 146:317–21.

—— "Writings of Bernard Mandeville: A Bibliographic Survey," *Journal of English and German Philology* (1921), 20:419–67.

Keohane, Nannerl O. "Nonconformist Absolutism in Louis XIV's France: Pierre Nicole and Denis Veiras," *Journal of the History of Ideas* (1974), 35:579–597.

Krailsheimer, A. J. *Studies in Self-Interest: Descartes to La Bruyere.* London: Oxford University Press, 1968.

Kramnick. Isaac. *Bolingbroke and his Circle: The Politics of Nostalgia in the Age of Walpole,* Cambridge, Mass.: Harvard University Press, 1968.

Lamprecht, S. P. "The Fable of the Bees," *The Journal of Philosophy* (1926), 23:561–79.

Larkin, Paschal. *Property in the Eighteenth Century.* London: Cook University Press, 1930.

Lecler, Joseph. "Liberalisme Economique et Libre Pensée au XXIII Siècle: Mandeville et la Fables des Abeilles." *Etudes* (1937), 230:629–40.

Letwin, William. *The Origins of Scientific Economics: English Economic Thought 1660–1776.* Garden City, N.Y.: Doubleday, 1963.

Levy, Anthony, *French Moralists.* Oxford: Clarendon Press, 1964.

Lipson, E. *The Economic History of England*, vols. 2–3. London: A. & C. Black, 1931.

Loftis, John. *Comedy and Society from Congreve to Fielding*. Stanford, Calif.: Stanford University Press, 1959.

—— *The Politics of Drama in Augustan England*. London: Oxford University Press, 1963.

Lovejoy, Arthur O. *Reflections on Human Nature*. Baltimore, Md.: Johns Hopkins University Press, 1961.

MacKay, Agnes Ethel. *La Fontaine and His Friends*. London: Garstove Press, 1972.

Marshall, M. Dorothy. *London Life in the Eighteenth Century*. New York: Capricorn Books, 1965.

Maxwell, J. C. "Ethics and Politics in Mandeville," *Philosophy* (1951), 26:240–52.

McGuire, J. E. "Bayle's Conception of Nature," *Journal of the History of Ideas* (1972), 33:523–33.

McPherson, Thomas S. "The Development of Bishop Butler's Ethics," *Philosophy* (1948, 1949), 23:316–30; 24:3–21.

Monro, Hector. *The Ambivalence of Bernard Mandeville*. London: Oxford University Press, 1975.

Moore, Cecil. "Shaftesbury and the Ethical Poets in England, 1700–1760," *PMLA* (1916), vol. 21.

Moore, John Robert. *Daniel Defoe: Citizen of the Modern World*. Chicago: University of Chicago Press, 1958.

Moore, W. G. *La Rochefoucauld: His Mind and Art*. London: Oxford University Press, 1969.

Morize, André. *L'apologie du luxe au XVIII siècle et le Mondain de Voltaire, etude critique sur le Mondain et ses sources*. Paris, 1909.

Mossner, Ernest C. *Bishop Butler and the Age of Reason*. New York: Macmillan, 1936.

Nishiyama, Chaiki. "The Theory of Self-Love." Dissertation, University of Chicago, 1960.

Novak, Maximillan E. *Defoe and the Nature of Man*. London: Oxford University Press, 1963.

Olscamp, Paul J. *The Moral Philosophy of George Berkeley*. The Hague: Martinus Nijhoff, 1970.

Plumb, J. H. *The First Four Georges*. London: Batsford, 1956.

—— *The Growth of Political Stability in England*. Baltimore, Md.: Penguin Books, 1967.

—— *Sir Robert Walpole*. 2 vols. London: Cressat Press, 1956.

Pocock, J. G. A. *The Machiavellian Moment*. Princeton, N.J.: Princeton University Press, 1974.

—— *Politics, Language, and Time*. New York: Atheneum, 1973.

—— "Virtue and Commerce in the Eighteenth Century," *Journal of Interdisciplinary History* (1972), 3:119–34.

Popkin, Richard. *The History of Skepticism.* New York: Harper and Row, 1964.

Popkin, Richard. "The Skeptical Precursors of David Hume," *Philosophy and Phenomenological Research* (1955), 16:61–71.

Portus, Garnet V. *Caritas Anglicana.* London: A. R. Mowbray, 1912.

Price, Martin. *To the Palace of Wisdom: Studies in Order and Energy from Dryden to Blake.* Garden City, N.Y.: Doubleday, 1964.

Primer, Irwin. "Introduction." *Fable of the Bees.* New York: Capricorn Books, 1962.

Primer, Irwin, ed. *Mandeville Studies: New Explorations in the Art and Thought of Dr. Bernard Mandeville.* The Hague: Martinus Nijhoff, 1975.

Raymond, Marcel. Du Jansenisme à la morale de intérêt," *Mercure de France* (1957), pp. 238–55.

Realey, C. B. *Early Opposition to Walpole: 1720–1727.* Lawrence, Kan.: University of Kansas Press, 1931.

Rich, Gertrude V. B. "Interpretation of Human Nature." Dissertation, Columbia University, 1935.

Robbins, Caroline. *The Eighteenth-Century Commonwealthman.* Cambridge, Mass.: Harvard University Press, 1959.

Robertson, J. M. *Essays Towards a Critical Method.* London: T. F. Unwin, 1889.

Robinson, Howard. *Bayle: The Skeptic.* New York: Columbia University Press, 1931.

Rogers, A. K. "The Ethics of Mandeville," *International Journal of Ethics* (1925), 36:1–17.

Rosenberg, Nathan. "Mandeville and Laissez-Faire," *Journal of the History of Ideas* (1963), 29:183–96.

Rothkrug, Lionel. *Opposition to Louis XIV: The Political and Social Origins of the French Enlightenment.* Princeton, N.J.: Princeton University Press, 1965.

Rude, George. *Hanoverian London.* Berkeley, Calif.: University of California Press, 1971.

Schatz, Albert. *L'Indiviudalisme economique et social.* Paris: Libraire Armand Colin, 1907.

—— "Bernard de Mandeville (contribution a l'étude des origines du liberalisme economique)," *Vierteljahreschift fur Social- und Wirtschaftsgeshichte* (1903), 1:434–80.

Schneider, Louis. "Mandeville as Forerunner of Modern Sociology," *Journal of History and Behavioral Sciences* (1964), 10:25–37.

Scott, William Robert. *Francis Hutcheson.* New York: Augustus M. Kelley, 1966; first published 1900.

Scott-Taggart, M. J. "Mandeville: Cynic or Fool," *Philosophical Quarterly* (1966), 16:221–32.

Selby-Bigge, L. A. "Introduction." *British Moralists,* vol. 1. New York: Dover Publications, 1965; first published 1897.

Shea, John. "Introduction." *Aesop Dressed*. Los Angeles: Augustine Reprint Society, No. 120, 1966.

Skarsten, A. Keith. "Nature in Mandeville," *Journal of English and Germanic Philology* (1954), 53:562–68.

Smith, LeRoy W. "Fielding and Mandeville: The War Against Virtue," *Criticism* (1961), 3:7–15.

Spengler, Joseph J. "Veblen and Mandeville Contrasted," *Weltwirtschaftlichs Archiv* (1959), 82–83:35–67.

Stephen, Leslie. *English Thought in the Eighteenth Century*, vols. 1–2. New York: Harcourt, Brace and World, 1962; first published 1876.

Stromberg, R. N. *Religious Liberalism in Eighteenth Century England*. London: Oxford University Press, 1954.

Suits, Conrad. "The Meaning of the Fable of the Bees." Dissertation, University of Chicago, 1961.

Sykes, Norman. *Church and State in England in the Eighteenth Century*. Conn.: Anchor Books, 1934.

Taveneaux, René. *Jansenisme et Politique*. Paris: Armand Colin, 1965.

Taylor, O. H. *Economics and Liberalism*. Cambridge, Mass.: Harvard University Press, 1955.

Taylor, W. L. *Francis Hutcheson and David Hume as Predecessors of Adam Smith*. Durham, N.C.: Duke University Press, 1965.

Tucker, G. S. L. *Progress and Profit in British Economic Thought 1650–1850*. London: Cambridge University Press, 1960.

Turbeville, A. S. *English Men and Manners in the Eighteenth Century*. London: Oxford University Press, 1929.

Vichert, Gordon S. "Bernard Mandeville and A Dissertation upon Drunkenness," *Notes and Queries* (1964), 209: 288–92.

—— "Some Recent Mandeville Attributions," *Philological Quarterly* (1966), 45:459–63.

Vickers, Douglas. *Studies in Theory of Money, 1690–1776*. Philadelphia: Chilton, 1959.

Viner, Jacob. *The Long View and the Short*. Glencoe, Ill.: Free Press, 1958.

—— *Studies in the Theory of International Trade* New York: Harper Brothers, 1937.

—— "Intellectual History of Laissez-Faire," *Journal of Law and Economics* (1960), 3:45–70.

—— "Introduction to Bernard Mandeville, A Letter to Dion." In *The Long View and the Short*, pp. 332–42. Glencoe, Ill. Free Press, 1958.

—— "Power versus Plenty as Objectives of Foreign Policy in the 17th and 18th Centuries," *World Politics* (1948), 1:277–306.

—— "Satire and Economics in the Augustan Age of Satire." In Harry Knight Miller, Eric Rothstein, G. S. Rousseau, eds., *The Augustan Milieu*. New York: Oxford University Press, 1970.

Watt, Ian. *The Rise of the Novel*. Berkeley, Calif.: University of California Press, 1957.

Whateley, Richard, *Introductory Lectures on Political Economy*. London, 1832.

Wilde, Norman. "Mandeville's place in English Thought," *Mind* (1898), 7:219–32.

Willey, Basil. *The Eighteenth Century Background*. Boston: Beacon Press, 1940.

Williams, Kathleen. *Jonathan Swift and the Age of Compromise*. Lawrence: University of Kansas Press, 1958.

Wolcott, Robert. *English Politics in the Early Eighteenth Century*. Cambridge, Mass.: Harvard University Press, 1956.

Yarrow, P. J. *A Literary History of France: The Seventeenth Century 1600–1715*. New York: Barnes and Noble, 1967.

Young, James D. "Mandeville: A Popularizer of Hobbes," *Modern Language Notes* (1959), 74:10–13.

# Index

121